# Praise for *Tarot fo*

"*Tarot for Troubled Times* is a powerful and poignant spiritual handbook for breaking through self-limiting belief systems and stirring hope and awakening to new personal discoveries. Filled with journaling prompts, affirmations, and Tarot-reading spreads to deal with depression, anxiety, grief, and addiction, this book will show you how to work through your own fears and inner shadowscapes, and break detrimental cycles. Shaheen Miro and Theresa Reed will inspire you to believe in your own magic. Heartfelt, encouraging, and beautifully written, *Tarot for Troubled Times* is a book of healing and personal evolution."

—**Benebell Wen**, author of *Holistic Tarot*

"Get ready to do some deep and powerful inner work with this book. Miro and Reed do not pull any punches. They hold a mirror up to the reader in a way that is both empowering and challenging but much needed. *Tarot for Troubled Times* goes beyond Tarot 101 to the core of who we are, our energy as Tarot readers, and what we can allow our lives to become. Through personal insights, rituals, meditations, and reflective exercises, the authors lead us on a supportive journey through self-discovery and Tarot card exploration. *Tarot for Troubled Times* is a treasure for any Tarot reader or student."

—**Ethony Dawn**, author of *Your Tarot Court*

"It's sometimes a little disheartening to see the saccharine 'love and light' posts all over the internet. Sometimes, you are stuck in the dark and twisties, and you need someone to meet you there, take your hand, and show you the way out. This is the book for those times. Miro and Reed show you how to welcome in the shadow side of life, give you tools to deal with it, and teach you how to embrace it, make it a shield or a weapon, and walk forward with confidence. This book is a safe space for those who struggle and isn't arrogant enough to try to force a smile on your faces. This is a real, honest handbook for peace of mind, and I'm thrilled that it's in the world."

—**Melissa Cynova**, author of *Tarot Elements* and *Kitchen Table Tarot*

"Are you ready to be empowered? Like Spirit speaking directly to you, Miro and Reed here share many paths to intentional, energy healing. Discover how healing yourself heals the world; how honoring yourself honors life. Through self-questioning and practices that are focused and enhanced by Tarot spreads, rituals, affirmations, birth and year energies, and elemental tools, this empowerment journey will be profound and deeply meaningful."

—**Mary K. Greer**, author of *Who Are You in the Tarot?*

"*Tarot for Troubled Times* is a brilliant look at how to work with the sacred art of Tarot and divination to support ourselves during the tough times—when we need the gifts of Tarot the most! Reed and Miro do a beautiful job of walking the reader through the basics that they need to know in order to get started. Then they address a host of situations that are stressful, frustrating, and downright troubling in a manner that is practical, calm, compassionate, and full of wisdom. Everyone interested in Tarot—professional reader and enthusiastic amateur alike—needs to have this book on their shelves."

—**Briana Saussy**, author of *Making Magic: Weaving Together the Everyday and the Extraordinary*

"*Tarot for Troubled Times* is an ally, a guide for us to understand our shadow, our inner wisdom, and the voice of the Tarot. This is the sort of book I've needed in the past without knowing it—a comprehensive guide for Tarot as a tool and resource to process and grow. Both Miro and Reed's light shines through in this book, allowing us to use the tools and symbols of the Tarot to lend a more delicate ear to our shadow, self, and needs. Through shadow work, magic, healing, the archetypes of the Tarot, and collective work through activism, this book guides you into harnessing your fullest self, even in the hardest times. A true gift that any mystic, witch, or Tarot reader deserves and one that everyone needs."

—**Gabriela Herstik**, author of *Inner Witch: A Modern Guide to the Ancient Craft*

"*Tarot for Troubled Times* is exactly what we all need right now. It's not a book on Tarot—it's a book on living, using the Tarot as a tool to deepen our understanding of ourselves and compassion for others. Smart, sharp, and kind, this book is a crucial navigational tool for a tumultuous era."

—**Courtney Weber**, author of *Tarot for One: The Art of Reading for Yourself* and *The Morrigan: Celtic Goddess of Magick and Might*

"*Tarot for Troubled Times* is just what the spiritual doctor ordered for our current energetic climate! A significant guide for modern times, it offers the powerful antidotes that can help us effectively cope with the turmoil of our inner and outer worlds. This book has deepened my relationship with Tarot in an innovative way and has sharpened my lens on how I can use this intuitive tool medicinally for myself and others."

—**Tatianna Morales**, creator of Tatianna Tarot

"*Tarot for Troubled Times* is a treasure to anyone interested in blooming in the face of shadow. Far more than your standard instructional Tarot guide, this is a book of hope, of healing, and of insight. Filled with rituals, meditations, journal prompts, and lessons on the Tarot, this book will leave you feeling whole, validated, and magical."

—**Lisa Marie Basile**, author of *Light Magic for Dark Times* and *Wordcraft*

"Reed and Miro's *Tarot for Troubled Times* is a truly beautiful and essential book for anyone who desires to take their Tarot practice to a deeper level. This book encourages us to look to the Tarot as a North Star for the times we live in and to open our arms to the hard, the scary, and the confusing aspects of life. Filled with helpful tools, beautiful examples, and guiding prompts to support readers on their path, *Tarot for Troubled Times* is part of a missing link in the canon of Tarot books—one that invites us to embrace the mud on the path to the lotus rather than try to bypass it."

—**Lindsay Mack**, creator of *Tarot for the Wild Soul*

"*Tarot for Troubled Times* manages to be a primer on shadow work, Tarot, and magick for the collective and the personal all at once while also digging deep and providing plenty of information for seasoned readers and magickal practitioners. The book manages to stay empowering and uplifting even though the topic at hand can get heavy on its own. Reed and Miro are both seasoned and skilled at what they do but what makes them both special is the heart that they put into their work. It's that heart that shines brightest in this book, not only leading us through navigating our own and the world's darkest waters but holding our hand and making us feel supported every step of the way."

—**Cassandra Snow**, author of *Queering the Tarot*

# TAROT FOR TROUBLED TIMES

# TAROT FOR TROUBLED TIMES

confront your shadow, heal your self, transform the world

SHAHEEN MIRO AND THERESA REED

This edition first published in 2019 by Weiser Books, an imprint of
Red Wheel/Weiser, LLC
With offices at:
65 Parker Street, Suite 7
Newburyport, MA 01950
www.redwheelweiser.com



ISBN: 978-1-57863-655-6
Library of Congress Cataloging-in-Publication Data available upon request.

Cover concept by Shaheen Miro
adapting the photograph "Countess Castiglione holding frame as mask"
by Adolphe Braun, 1811–1877 (in the collection of the Metropolitan Museum of Art, New York)
Interior by Kathryn Sky-Peck
Typeset in Myriad Pro

Printed in Canada
MAR
10 9 8 7 6 5 4 3 2

*Dedicated to those brave souls on the front line for positive change . . . we see you, honor you, and thank you!*

*Also, to Mary K. Greer, whose work with the Tarot Constellations inspired this book.*

# Table of Contents

## PART TWO. THE TAROT: A MIRROR ON THE SELF

*Now that we've gone deep enough in our personal work we are ready to confront the insight Tarot can provide.*

## PART THREE. THE WORLD: A FOCUS ON THE COLLECTIVE

*Take the pain you've experienced and use your story to inspire others, coming full circle like the World card of the Tarot deck. Take your broken heart and channel it into your art. Take the healing rituals you've learned and share them with others. Take the light that's inside of you and bring it outside to shine for all.*

# Introduction

*Look at how a single candle can both defy and define the darkness.*

—Anne Frank

The world has gone wild, exploding with so much noise . . . and this has been a long time coming. The social and political climate is something that many of us have grown weary of, and for those who are sensitive to the uncertainty in the world, it has been detrimental to their well-being. But know this: we're living in a time of profound shadow work. The paradigm is cracking, shifting, and revealing to us the fear, pain, and chaos that have been bubbling under the surface for lifetimes. Collectively and individually, we are being called to take action, to face the shadow and instigate radical change.

We can be part of the solution.

Over the years, we've had countless conversations with people who feel lost, hopeless, and are wondering what can be done to heal this world . . . and themselves. Those conversations led to a class and, now, to this book that you are holding in your hands.

*Tarot for Troubled Times* isn't just another Tarot book. Instead, it's a handbook for personal evolution, social justice, and healing.

In *Tarot for Troubled Times*, we are going to show you how to work with your shadow so that you can liberate yourself from old patterns and limiting beliefs. You will learn how to make peace with personal archetypes such as the victim and the bully so that you can operate in the world as a positive, proactive force for good.

We'll begin by examining personal fears and shadows. Through introspection and meditation, you'll face the dark and find the sources of light within yourself. This crucial first step lays the foundation for our work with the Tarot.

From there, you'll learn the archetypes of the Major Arcana and how to befriend your shadow and heal yourself. We'll also help you discover through affirmations, Tarot prescriptions, magical rituals, and other healing modalities healthy ways to find your voice and speak out so that you can become an ally and begin to do your greater work in the world.

Then, we'll begin exploring how the shadow shows up on the global stage. Once again, the Major Arcana will reveal what's happening in the world and how you can make a difference in a way that makes sense for your archetype. We'll also investigate practical ways to step up as an ally or leader so that you can learn how to shape policies and become an agent of change.

We're also going to look deeply at issues that have touched many of us at one time or another: death, grief, divorce, illness, addiction, and oppression. With a selection of mindful, introspective Tarot spreads, you'll learn how the Tarot constellations can help you rewrite your healing story and change your life.

Through this book, you will discover a different approach to Tarot, life, and self-empowerment. Even if you are not a Tarot card reader or have no intention of ever pulling cards for another person, this book will guide you to transform yourself so that you can change the world.

The goal of this book is to help you heal yourself—and the world. We are all in this together, and if each of us does the work, we can become powerful beyond belief.

At times, you may still feel enraged or helpless. Life may hand you problems that seem far greater than your ability to manage, or the world may seem to be falling apart faster than a wet paper towel. During these challenging times, Tarot is your friend. Like the Hermit's lamp, Tarot is the trusted ally that can guide you inward to the source of light and wisdom that is *you*.

*Tarot for Troubled Times* is a contribution to the light and empowerment of those brave seekers who wish to go deep into the conflict, excavate the shadow, and reveal the light. Now more than ever we need to discover our intrinsic gifts as we go into the world fortified and aware as radical beings of light for positive change.

—Shaheen Miro and Theresa Reed

PART ONE

# THE FOOL

## *A Focus on the Personal*

*Dear seeker and kind soul: you are about to embark on a journey that will change your life and quite possibly the world you live in.*

*In this section, you will be getting the tools you need so that you can begin taking that first brave step toward navigating our troubled times.*

# 1

# What's in Your Knapsack?

If you were about to spend a week deep in the wilderness, you probably wouldn't attempt it without the correct supplies, right? You'd want to bring a knapsack filled with all the essentials: a compass, knife, tent, dry clothes, canteen, and foodstuffs. These tools would help you survive if you were to encounter treacherous weather or wild animals.

Without these necessities, your adventure might take a dark turn.

You'd be a Fool.

But what about when you're dealing with the big, wild world closer to home? How do you cope when all you see in the media is doom and gloom? Do you suck it up and stuff your feelings behind a closed door that no one can reach? Or do you choose to numb yourself through drugs, alcohol, sex, or endless hours in front of the television? If these are the ways you are choosing to operate when turmoil strikes, you may be depleting your emotional gas tank and running on empty.

At some point, if you stay on this course, you're going to bottom out. You need the right tools to remain grounded, healthy, and happy no matter what is going on out there . . . or in your own life. Remember that ultimately what is happening *inside you* is what will dictate how you cope, manage, or take a stand in the world.

When you draw from your knapsack, or inner reserve, you fortify yourself against the rough terrain of the great wilderness of life. And you don't just survive . . . you thrive.

Maybe you've spent your whole life feeling like you're fighting an uphill battle, being met with continuous challenges, roads to nowhere, and endless surprises. Many others have, too. But there is a different way of living and being in the world—a spiritual way, led by the wisdom of your inner compass.

If you look at Tarot's Fool, you might notice he has a small backpack that he carries on a wand. The wand symbolizes magic, and that knapsack is filled with his past experiences as well as the tools he needs to move about freely. He can leap into the world with total confidence because on some level, he knows that he has the proper utensils to make magic happen.

What about you? What's in your knapsack?

Is it full of magical implements and practices that uplift and sustain you?

Or is your knapsack empty?

What if you could be certain the necessary rituals and utensils were there for you whenever you need them? Imagine how your life would look. Instead of operating out of fear, you'd be living with total freedom. Better yet, you might be inspired to step up and lead with boldness, and that is what the world needs in troubled times: fearless leaders with the resources to guide and uplift us all.

But you can only do and be that if you have the appropriate tools.

We're not talking about hammers and nails. Instead, we're looking at the spiritually oriented stuff such as meditation, Tarot, magical rites, and affirmations.

These devotional tools have helped people for centuries have calm, meaningful lives, even when the world felt unsafe. Here's the truth: we've been living in troubled times since humankind first figured out how to start a fire. Wars, violence, and tragedies have plagued us since the very beginning, so troubled times are nothing new—but neither are the practices in this book.

We're going to show you ways to work with ancient spiritual traditions and tools so that you can be the best version of yourself . . . no matter what is happening out there.

Instead of hobbling through life, your journey can look like something else: Golden light floods over your shoulders and fills you with a glow of freedom and certainty. Your steps are light and buoyant and ready for new terrain. Over your shoulder you carry a staff fixed with a small, red knapsack at one end. Bundled inside are the tools and implements you need to navigate any situation that might fall into your path.

Moving closer to the edge of uncertainty, your belly flutters with butterflies of anticipation. Great adventures have a funny way of filling us with wonder and trepidation—essential fuel to keep you moving.

Each step you take will hold the promise of possibility. Whether you stroll through peaceful meadows or find yourself negotiating rough, rocky terrain, with a bit of planning and commitment you'll be ready to meet whatever lies ahead. You might even blaze a few trails.

Before you cross the threshold into the wild stretches of unknown land, consider what you might bring to make your journey easier. Gather your awareness and sink your feet into the present moment. A successful adventure starts with intentional planning and preparation.

Finding your present coordinates gives you enough awareness to take your first steps confidently. So start by noticing where you are. What is the present state of your life? What are you missing? What do you have in abundance? Are you prepared for change?

The first thing to pack in your knapsack is a compass. You want to have a keen sense of direction, especially when you wander into uncharted territory. That compass is the difference between orienting yourself or being lost in space.

Each one of us is gifted with an internal navigation system as a means for traversing all the ups and downs of life. Deep inside of you is an unshakable knowing, your deeper wisdom, your truest voice, your intuition. This guiding force has always been there, waiting for you to trust, look, and listen.

Every step of the way holds a new challenge, a new possibility, and a chance to grow. Sometimes you will be met with challenges that you cannot change. You might be on a path with no other way but forward. Even if you cannot alter your present circumstances, you can still change your reaction to it. By using your internal compass and arming yourself with the proper tools, you'll find your way and thrive!

You can start by changing how you look at the world. If you're viewing the land before you with fear, you'll be sure to find fearsome things. Rather than meet this adventure with resistance, open yourself up. Be brave, curious, and willing to observe everything around you just as it is.

Close your eyes and take a deep breath down into your belly. Let it out slowly. Continue filling your body with deep, luscious breaths, exhaling each one slowly. When you start to feel settled, scan your body from head to toe. Notice any physical sensations. What is your body telling you? Listen to the sounds around you. What do you notice? As you continue breathing in and out, observe any thoughts that arise in your mind. Where does your brain go? Are you thinking about a random task, fretting over a problem, or do you feel anchored in the present moment? Open your eyes and look around you. What catches your eye? How does it make you feel? Are you rooted in the now or somewhere else?

Take a few more deep, conscious breaths. Orient yourself so that you face north. Even if you're not sure where it is, let your body find north. Once you are in position, plant your feet firmly on the ground, drawing energy up from the earth into your legs. Feel yourself becoming grounded, present, and fully in the world.

You're here—right where you are supposed to be. Know that, no matter where you are standing or what is happening in your world or the world, you can make a difference. You can be a formidable force for good.

Before you can throw yourself fully into that role, you must know the terrain and your abilities, and fill your knapsack with all the essential spiritual tools. This starts by going through the darkness and facing the shadows you find there! And that is just what we will do together.

One of the most important tools you'll need on this journey is a journal. A journal is a place to record your thoughts, feelings, readings, rituals, and experiences. Like a trusted friend, your journal will help you unpack issues, clear your emotions, harness your creativity, contemplate your life lessons, and understand yourself. A journal will give you support as you navigate the often treacherous terrain of the world you live in.

Journaling brings clarity and mindfulness, which set the foundation for healing, growth, and change. As you take time to record your life, you can begin to unravel the knots and liberate yourself from the bondage of limiting beliefs, old stories, pain, grief, and anger. As you make peace with those parts of yourself, you begin to develop compassion, the first step necessary for changing the world.

Your journal doesn't need to be fancy—even a plain notebook will do. Find one that you like and then begin.

• • • • • • • • • • • • • • • • • • • • • • • • • • • • • • • • • • • •

Before we go any further, take some time to journal around these prompts. Write whatever comes to mind. Let your feelings flow! Remain curious and open. Do not censor yourself. See what comes up for you. When you feel done, put it aside and review it a few weeks later—especially after you've worked through the other exercises in this book.

*Where do you feel stuck, blocked, or in pain?*

*Where do you feel good, whole, blessed, and in the flow?*

*If you could change any of this, what would that be?*

*What might that look like?*

*When have you felt afraid to speak up?*

*How do you hold yourself back?*

*In what ways do you lift other people up?*

*When have you contributed to oppression, either knowingly or unknowingly?*

*When have you felt oppressed? What was that like?*

*What does the word power mean to you?*

*When you think of inclusivity, what does that look like in your life? How might you create a more inclusive, welcoming world for people of color or other marginalized folks?*

Take your time with this. Do not judge yourself. Hold space for it. Take deep breaths.

Now . . . get ready to face your shadow and find the light.

# 2

# Shadow Dancing: Get Out of Limbo and Into Your Magic

Moment to moment, we find ways to be completely present, but as a whole, it becomes easy to slip into anxiety and depression . . . pondering the pain of the past or losing ourselves in the possibilities of the future. What's interesting is figuring out how to show up in all of our dripping, magical glory at the disco happening right here, right now!

That means dancing to every song and feeling every light burning as the mirror ball turns, finding the rhythm in the song . . . doing the dance, until the dance does you.

What are we talking about?

We are talking about being in the present moment with whatever is before us, around us, and, most importantly, within us. This includes all our dreams, desires, fears, and screwups. You cannot heal the pain or create the dream if you cannot be in the moment with *every part* of yourself as it is. And you cannot connect with the full message of Tarot unless you can look at all of you with clear eyes.

Changing your perspective is essential to becoming coherent and congruent with all your parts. If you're hitting the wall, losing your rhythm, or finding yourself in despair, then you've forgotten how big, magical, and vibrant you really are.

It's easy to give in to the small, paper-doll version of yourself—that icky part of you that believes you are only what you see in the mirror.

The truth is that's only one aspect of yourself . . . your shadow!

## *What Is the Shadow?*

Everyone has a subtle darkness that wraps around them like a soft, velvet cloak. This is your shadow, the part of you that is dark, rich, and fertile. It is the place where we lock our fears and insecurities, our monsters and demons. The shadow is that space within and around you where you feel abandoned, lost, and confused. It is that space where you feel completely out of control, poked and prodded by chaos and fear.

The dark is really the beginning and the end, the alpha and omega. The dark is the womb of creation, the tomb of destruction, and the cave of regeneration. You fall into the dark when you are stepping out of your box. You are pushed in the dark when you are growing beyond your personal limitations.

Deep inside every one of our psyches is this dark, murky spot. This is a place where we'd rather not tread. Instead, we prefer to shut the door, ignore it, and put our attention to love and light or whatever other pleasantries we'd rather present as ourselves.

Psychologist Carl Jung called this "the shadow," the part of ourselves that we don't like to face so we tend to avoid or hide it in some way. On the outside, we look fine, but on the inside, we're consumed by thoughts such as fear, jealousy, anger, perfectionism, or worse. We bury the ugly parts of ourselves, when in reality the shadow longs to be acknowledged.

If we focus only on the surface or the stuff that feels comfortable, our healing journey can go only so far. We must first confront those fears, emotions, weaknesses, and inner conflicts within ourselves if we wish to experience deep healing. We must come face-to-face with the shadow, that part of ourselves that is deeply wounded.

Disconnected from your empowering energy, the shadow grows stronger and thrives on your pain. Rather than interacting with life, you react. Reactionary living is acidic, corrosive, and destructive. That is not to say we can live without reaction. It is a human response and serves to keep us alert and alive. But we can learn to interact with the world by befriending experience—and still remaining safe.

By listening to your shadow, you discover that there is a whole other side of you: the bigger, brighter, and more luminous self hidden right there in the dark.

We are in troubled times that mark a pivotal shift in all our lives. It's a time of getting closer to our inner truth. Spirit has been calling you into action, asking you to lean in and go for a ride. Bravery and curiosity allow the road to rise up and meet you—filled with avenues of blessing and hurdles of learning. But, all in all, this road leads to fluid living.

In your intimate moments of inner voyage, you can hear your spirit whisper: *Are you ready to be empowered?*

Self-empowerment is beautiful concept. Finding an inner well of truth that can forever nourish you on the ride of life, through the good and bad, empowerment is your wild sister reminding you of your innate strengths and talents. She shows you how to hold space rather than dominate. You can be a force for good in the world when you stand in the circle of your personal empowerment. Stop trying to explain yourself or bring people over to your side. You have nothing to prove to anyone else. Just be you.

In a material world bent on power, we have confused personal strength with domination over our perceived opponents. This attempt to segregate, control, and draw lines in the sand has bred so much fear. But there is another way of being. Relinquish the need to dominate what is outside of you and learn to ride the tide of your personal power from within.

The real battle is the internal struggle. The state of your life is a holographic creation of the deeply held perspective within your consciousness. Before you start grappling with feelings of guilt and shame, stop! You are not responsible for all the painful things you've been through or are going through, but you can choose to receive these experiences. You have choice!

Do you accept the beauty and the pain with open arms of perfect love and perfect trust?

If you can take in the messy parts, just as much as you can embrace the awesome, then you can begin to create magic in your life. You can lay the shadow to rest, feeding the hungry ghosts of your pain and accepting the gifts of your fear. Become present with the feelings and desires that well up within you. Let the experience move you, inspire you, and transform you, rather than control you.

When we feel contempt for an experience, we cut ourselves off from the opportunity to grow, thrive, and become aligned. So often we forgo the messages coded within our pain. Pain is a reminder to pay attention. It is a deep call from your spirit to return to wellness. We all know what this looks like—it appears as a loss of vitality, strength, confidence, and commitment.

It doesn't sound fun, does it? But we *all* do it . . . all the time. Numbing out might seem easy at first, but the shadow grows longer and wider until it becomes a pervasive darkness.

When something has you plugged in to pain, instead of ignoring or disregarding it, approach it with openness. Be willing to find out the why. Opposition will only create deeper fragmentation. You're leeching away your power every time you step out of the present moment where the hurt and the beauty live.

Your shadow holds your pain and your fear. Fear is a sign you are in the cycle of change. You know you are undergoing some interstellar transformation when you acknowledge your pain and face your fear.

Each moment, and in each experience, you encounter a central question. It delves into what you will accept, how you will feel, what you choose to think. It explores your needs, desires, and who you are or are becoming. It looks directly at where you are wounded. And this most profound question is *what empowers you?*

Each moment offers you a choice about how you will act, interact, or react. Each experience asks the question. This is so profound and so healing. Most people are looking for permission to be, think, feel, and live. Whom do you think you need permission from? Remind yourself that this permission comes from within.

Go deeper and ask yourself: What part of me is this painful experience validating? What is my fear trying to show me?

On some level, you've conjured this unique experience where pain, fear, and healing all move together. When something hurts, we are begging for change and an opportunity to grow. Wounds can validate us and reveal how much progress we've actually made. Do you want to take the leap into transformation?

Slip into the dance. Take your shadow by the hand. Let the story unravel. You are the *creator* of your story, not just the character. If you can be present and honest with yourself, the song will change, the story will shift, and the magic will begin.

The shadow can feel dark, fearful, taunting, and deadly. She can seduce you into anger, fear, pain, and sadness. Coursing through your veins, she can feel like hot, surging lava. But your shadow not only holds the unacknowledged, unloved, and unhealed parts of yourself; she also carries within her these beautiful blessings. Her biggest gift is the gift of choice.

Befriending the shadow places creating your life back in your hands. She only feels limiting because she holds the parts of you that have been ignored for so long. She can look like anything: the part of you that feels helpless, the part of you that fears commitment, the part of you that believes money is elusive. But rather than letting your shadow well up inside and come out as reaction, you can find stillness and silence within her. Retreat into a space where you can ask the questions that give you choice:

*What does your shadow look like? Is it big and scary? Or is it a tight, constricted little fist that leaves no room for the light?*

*Where do you feel aggravated by others? Is it a quality you yourself have?*

*What are your shadow beliefs?*

*What are the parts of yourself that bring you shame when you think about them?*

*What are you repressing or rejecting? What are you covering up with woo-woo metaphysical babble?*

Always go deeper and ask her . . . *why?*

Retreating into your sacred space can help you communicate with your shadow. Constructive time together lessens the deadly blow of force that she brings when a crack opens for her to creep through. She is looking for approval, validation, and, when left to her own devices, proof that she has a reason to be who she is.

Working on the shadow is one of the hardest challenges you'll ever take on, but this effort will free you. You'll have a deeper understanding of yourself and the patterns that create negativity and self-destructive or limiting beliefs and behaviors in your life.

Let's begin the process of excavating your light by slipping into the dark where your shadow can reveal herself.

## *Slipping into Shadows and Navigating the Dark*

*Shadow is the means by which bodies display their form. The forms of bodies could not be understood in detail but for shadow.*

—Leonardo da Vinci

Life is a series of cycles. There are ups and downs, a back and forth. You may sense a strange feeling of limbo that you think will never break. There are times when things feel hot and arid. And then there are the times when you are caught in the storm. The most memorable of times are when you are in the dark.

The Tower card in the Tarot is a symbol of the dark. The illustration shows a huge tower looming over the ocean—mighty, strong, tall, and indestructible—yet the foundation is cracked. The top is being struck by lightning. The invincible monolith is destroyed, and it topples into the waves. It symbolizes the ending of beliefs posing as facts—and the edge of life as you know it!

You must learn to dance in the dark. If you stand still and make no move or sound, you will eventually *become* a shadow. You've seen people who've been consumed by the dark, letting fears, addiction, pain, and psychosis take their lives.

Dance with your shadows, move through the dark, and marry the night. The dark is one big, crazy disco. You may not always like the song, but if you let the rhythm of intuition guide you, you'll find your feet moving to the next beat. Sometimes you have to slow grind, sometimes you have to waltz, and sometimes you have to just sway in the dark!

The dark, the unknown, the night, the chaos . . . it isn't your enemy, no matter how much you misunderstand or fight it. You can discover it is a friend. It will test your limits, push you to the breaking point, and show you what you're really made of.

Remember, even in the blackness, you have a little spark of light inside of you. So close your eyes and glow in the dark. Listen to the beat, and move yourself through to the end.

You may fear the darkness, but what if you learn to touch it?

You feel strong when you keep your composure during hard times. You sigh with relief when you push through anger, fists and jaw clenched, as if you are bracing yourself through an earthquake. It's easy to avoid what feels terrifying . . . to avoid the unknown. But why do you fear your darkness? When did feeling become bad?

Did someone tell you that the dark is bad?

Were you spooked as a child by the things that went bump in the night or the boogeyman that lived under the bed?

What are your shadow beliefs?

They may include thoughts such as:

*I don't matter.*

*I'm not enough.*

*No one cares . . . why bother?*

*Everyone else must come first.*

*I wish I could be someone else.*

*Why do they get all the attention and not me?*

*I can't forgive myself/them. This must make me a bad person.*

Do *not* judge yourself for having these feelings. Just pay attention to how you feel and ask yourself without shame or blame: What's behind this? Why am I feeling this?

These feelings did not come about on their own. Instead, they grow from experiences and events that happened long ago. Much of the time, these shadow beliefs can be traced back to our childhood. As crystal healer Diane Bloom says: "We all need therapy because every one of us had a childhood."

Perhaps when you were young, you were punished for "being bad." Maybe you hit your sibling in a fit of anger. Or maybe you didn't do your homework because it was boring. In these situations, your parents or teacher might have criticized you, labeled you a brat, or called you lazy. In some cases, you may have received punishment.

Other times, when you "behaved"—for example, by being quiet—you were rewarded and called "good."

This disapproval/approval cycle, combined with our need to feel secure and loved, is what creates the shadow. All of the "good" parts become the mask we show to the world, while the other "bad" parts get packed away in an internal closet and are rarely revealed outside.

We spend so much time trying to avoid the difficult. Is this born from our need for control?

You may fear that if you touch the darkness, you will fade like a drop in the ocean into a strange realm of eternal night, never to return again. But why do you care? Maybe there's really a great carnival raging somewhere in the darkness, waiting for you to step through your shadow.

Some people get lost in their shadow. You can be consumed by your own darkness. Depression can clutch you like the fatal talons of a hawk and never let you go. Anger can burn you from the inside out. All of these lower emotions can eat away at you if you let them. People become prisoners of their darkness because they give all their power to their fears.

Befriend the night.

Marry your own darkness. Learn to dance with the chaos and the uncertainty. Learn to be with your unlovable parts. A wound cannot heal if you fear looking at it. You have to assess the damage. If there are really monsters brewing in the dark, do they disappear when you close your eyes?

Your greatest fear could become your greatest friend.

We learn through opposition the strength of our character. You can't live in a vacuum. You have to take in the light and the dark, so that you can really see who you are. We are all the interplay of light and shadow; without one you can't have the other. That's balance.

There is an art to taking good photographs. A talented photographer understands the play of light and darkness and how to use both to their advantage to capture a spectacular image. And as all good artists know: if you learn the rules, you can break them.

Be bold, be brave, and step out there and walk the middle ground. Let your darkness show you something you never knew before—or never wanted to know. If you let it consume you, you become numb, you lose passion, and without passion, nothing can live.

Passion is the lifeblood of everything.

Passion is the sun to the plants. Passion is the fire in the hearth. Passion is the love in the heart. Passion is an invisible force that lives inside of each thing, and when you activate that energy, like a spark it springs to life and creates beauty. You cannot have passion if you cannot feel. And you can't feel if you are afraid to step into the unknown.

Passion begins with curiosity.

You may say, "Well, how do I befriend my shadow?"

It's simple: go there. What are you afraid of? If you fear talking to strangers, take that feeling deeper and explore why. Maybe that's why you've been unable to meet a partner. Maybe at your core you fear rejection. Take the power back, muster the strength, and go talk to someone.

So, you don't know how to get past that anxiety. Leap before you think. Those in-between spaces are where curiosity lives. That is the instinctual part of you, devoid of ego and preconceived notions. You act from your center, where light and shadow come together like two great streams flowing into a river.

## *Lesson in Letting Go*

Shaheen can look back to a very interesting lesson in letting go:

"When I was in foundations drawing my freshman year, my professor made the class do a very interesting drawing exercise. He had all of us take out a sheet of paper and a piece of charcoal. We covered the white paper in charcoal, until there was nothing but a thick fuzzy black canvas. And then he projected on the screen in front of us abstract images of black with small slices of white throughout.

We were instructed to copy each image exactly as it appeared, by erasing the charcoal from our page to allow slivers of white to peek through the black. The entire time, we had no clue what we were doing. We just had to trust. It all looked like random shapes of black and white, of light and shadow, woven together.

Once we got to the last slide, sculpting away at our page, as instructed, he asked us to stop and look at the page before us for a few seconds. I felt defeated because all I saw before me was a jumbled mess. Then he asked us to rotate the page, until finally he said stop. The orientation was changed, and so was the image I held.

Holding the page with a new perspective and seeing with new eyes, I found an entire drawing of a man crouched over, holding a skull in his hand in a contemplative pose. Moments before, the image was not there. I had created this picture entirely from an undefined place of discovery. An abstract collection of shapes and shadows turned into a cohesive drawing with nothing more than a flip of a page.

What a mind-blowing experience that was. It felt enlightening. I had let go of control and moved with the unknown, letting the dark instruct me.

What if we learn to live in a state of curiosity and see things from alternate views? Changing orientations to look at things upside down and sideways—maybe even backward—shaking fear's hand, and remaining curious about the fertile dark where things are limitless—this is the womb of creation.

As I sit here writing, the sky is alive with rain and thunder. She is purging, brewing, and renewing herself and the world beneath her. So much magic comes from such moments of release. The cleansing waters wash away the pain and fear and reveal the beautiful light that lives within. Falling rain always signals to me a profound change taking place, and yet it reminds me to honor the deeply held forces within. Inasmuch as they can renew, they can also destroy.

But isn't destruction just another word for rebirth?

I have been in a personal storm lately. All my parts are coming undone to reveal the weak spots and the strong points that live within. As one thing is exposed, I can acknowledge it and move through to the next thing. In this personal dance of light and shadow I find comfort in learning what I am made of.

In these telling moments that push you to your edge, strengths are revealed.

Cracking open reveals what fills you out. A slippery, multilayered world lives inside you—a world of pain, grace, memory, experience, fear, and perspective where the light and shadow cradle your personal power.

Unexpected changes fizzle up fears and prompt introspection. Old beliefs and dreams might fall away, but they reveal the smooth, robust, and luscious flesh of possibility. New intentions to nourish are allowed to germinate. This is inner alchemy where you purge and part with to find your grace.

Can you open your arms wide and be nourished by the falling waters of change?

## *The Alchemical Path of Expressing the Shadow Self*

Life can seem like a black hole trying to suck you in. You feel exhausted, defeated, and unable to fight through another day. You want to crawl back into bed and forget about the world that is demanding something from you. We get it, babe! Things can seem really bad, and you don't see how you can make it any better.

Many of you can relate to those moments of feeling cloudy and unbalanced. We all find ourselves feeling out of sync with life and completely deaf to the wisdom of our inner voice.

Slipping out of awareness and balance is something that society has programmed us to do oh so well. Put your nose to the grindstone. Get to work. Be seen, not heard. Shut up and don't ask questions. Never cause a rift. Be normal. Do as you're told. Work and then die. On and on goes a fierce pursuit to distance our spirit from our waking life. No wonder most of us walk around unhealthy, unhappy, and confused.

This is not some kind of blame game or a declaration of martyrdom. We are speaking from personal experience and the countless stories of so many people. But this status quo can be changed when you decide to face your fears and take back your power!

Give yourself a big hug and kiss. Throw a little tantrum on the floor. Break something if you need to. Call into work. Cancel your plans. Cry your eyes out. Eat a big vat of ice cream. *Own your darkness!*

Cultivating personal awareness through self-care is an essential component for happiness. Whether you are a spiritual person or just someone who aspires to live healthy and whole, it is important to consider your relationship with yourself. At the core of all personal growth is the need for right relationship.

Shaheen describes how he navigates this terrain:

**"**I am always in self-exploration mode, trying to understand what gifts are hidden deep within my soul, my shadow, and under all the baggage that exists from daily living. There are always series of ups and downs. Learning to navigate them can be tricky business. No one has it all figured out, but openness and curiosity are key.

Sadly, we have created a society that does not uphold deep, personal exploration and introspection. Rather than look for the root of dis-ease, we want a quick fix or, worse, to just ignore the pain that is festering. Eventually the wounds become too painful to ignore, and we look for relief.

## *Seeing Stories of Pain and Healing*

Shaheen has experienced many life stories:

//As an intuitive, I have witnessed many profound tales of pain and healing. Some of them are my own experiences, but others are from the many people I have worked with. What I have found is this deep longing for wholeness and wellness. But wholeness only comes when we shine a light on the pain, move into it, and desire to make changes.

People want relief and release from cycles of hell and troubled times they are faced with. Looking out at the world, the fear and pain can be debilitating. But the process of healing begins within, and we must learn to venerate the shadow parts of ourselves because that is where the true work starts. Let's step out of the magical thinking complex where we cover our wounds with crystals, prayers, and lots of positive affirmations. We need to start at the foundation—the rich, fertile soil of our shadow.

Tools are valuable. You're going to learn all about tools and techniques to create change in your life. But these are just the avenues for going in. The tool is the key, and the wound is the entry point.

Ceremony, energy work, and self-exploration are cornerstones for your personal practice. The process of healing and building a more congruent self is an ongoing and intentional step in the right direction. Our practice helps us actively participate in our recovery. But the real secret to spiritual cleansing, clearing, and healing is having a dialogue with the self!

To begin the deep work of cultivating right relationship with yourself, you have to face your shadow. To create long-lasting shifts and changes in your spirit, your mental/emotional state, and your life, you have to be willing to stop, get still, and listen to what is happening inside.

Without acknowledging the wounds that make up your shadow, spiritual tools become nothing more than Band-Aids. We've grown discontent with this approach in the spiritual community because it doesn't create lasting change. If you sew up the superficial damage without removing the shrapnel, eventually it festers back to the surface. And it's usually not very pretty.

Now there is benefit to the short-term relief because it gives you a glimpse of clarity and hope. But you want to heal and fortify yourself so you can move from feeling powerless to powerful.

Exercises such as visualizations, rituals, journaling questions, and prompts can help with the process. They provide a gentle push to explore who you are, what is happening in your head and heart, and why. You have to pull out the roots or the weed will return.

Begin by holding space for yourself: a safe environment to be open, vulnerable, and completely naked with everything you feel and have experienced. You don't have to hide your pain anymore; your wounds are what makes you strong. Your pain helps you clarify your purpose. Isolation and loneliness can breed victim mentality and keep you in these limiting cycles.

So how do you battle the long, dark shadow when it comes around?

Stop fighting! That's the first step. When you are in the dark about something, completely confused, or feeling sad, look at it as a gift of insight, not your enemy. These dark, off-kilter moments are your spirit's way of saying, "Hey, you've disconnected from your goodness and grace. Come back now!"

Like a fish out of water, you begin to feel every fiber of your being shrivel up with deprivation, starving from a lack of love. You find yourself ravenous for spiritual and emotional sustenance. This is because our natural state is to be in grace, in the moment, in fluidity, not in this dense, dark, disconnected, and rigid reality we have claimed as the truth.

## *Finding the Roots of Resistance*

Slip into that deep space inside of you that feels lost, broken, and in trauma. Breathe awareness into your body, your head, and your heart. Allow yourself to feel what is happening down below in the spaces that you've locked away from the rest of the world—whether it is out of fear, guilt, or shame. If you can be with yourself in these uncomfortable places, you can untangle the knots, release the resistance, and set the hungry ghosts of your shadow free.

When you are seeking to change your circumstance, look deeper and see what is feeding it. With simple practices, we can find momentary relief from some of the heaviness and pain. But if you are enmeshed in a limiting situation, then the only real solution is to work your way out of it.

Taking time to get really deep, begin asking, Why?

Once you befriend your shadow parts, your pain, you find yourself dancing in the dark. You move into the sacred communion with your light and your shadow—born of rhythm and fluidity. The shadow is not bad; rather it is the rejection of the shadow that causes pain.

You might need time to make this happen. Be gentle with yourself, and work on having compassion. Shame, fear, and guilt are never good for inspiring healing. We might need to work on the superficial for a bit until we can crack that exterior and go inward to where the juicy power lives.

Invite yourself to cultivate right relationship for yourself by holding space. Make the room to listen quietly without reacting to what you are really feeling.

Ask yourself: What is motivating my fear? (Instead of, What am I afraid of?)

Ask yourself: What is causing my pain? (Instead of, What hurts?)

When something feels bad, then let it feel bad. Don't talk yourself out of it, and don't guilt yourself for not feeling like sunshine, rainbows, and a big cloud of glitter. It's okay. You can't lie to yourself about how you feel.

Take some time to express to your shadow all that you feel. Be open, honest, and candid with your shadow. Express your deepest sensations of pain, disappointment, and even resentment.

*What do you feel about your shadow?*

*What has she done to you?*

*Where have you felt held back in your life?*

*What have you missed out on?*

*Why and how do you feel small in your life?*

Openly express this to your shadow self.

Really reach out to your shadow with bravery and curiosity. Accept that she is here reminding you to go deeper, love harder, and flow more gracefully.

Gently ask her: Why are you here?

Listen for her answer.

Take some time and meditate around these questions:

*Can you remember a time when you acted out and were punished?*

*How were feelings handled in your family?*

*Were you encouraged to express them freely or were you told that certain emotions were not "nice"?*

*Can you recall a time when you were shut down for expressing your needs?*

*How did that feel?*

*Were your parents affectionate . . . or not?*

*What did it feel like when you experienced disapproval from an authority figure? How about when you experienced approval?*

*Which emotions were considered "bad" in your family? Which emotions were considered "good"?*

*How do you express anger, fear, depression, or other so-called negative emotions today?*

*What does your shadow tell you?*

*Why have you been afraid? Or angry? Or lonely?*

*Ask your shadow how she has grown so big.*

*Ask your shadow how you can help her heal.*

Journal your answers and notice what you feel. Be gentle with yourself. Then look again with new, softer eyes, and ask yourself: *Why have I neglected my shadow?*

This process could take on any form. You can imagine your shadow as a figure sitting next to you. The shadow could even pull up a chair in front of you for a one-on-one verbal conversation. Just let out how you feel in response to your shadow, and she will listen. Write letters or journal. Finger paint with your shadow or collage or dance. And as your shadow listens to you, you must listen to her.

When you're done getting out the angst, take a deep breath, put on something that feels sexy, and remember this:

*You are fucking powerful!*

You are *really* powerful, more powerful than you know. You are a walking mystical being filled with so much light and magic that you could blow the roof off the world. So don't shy away from your darkness, and *never* shy away from your *light*.

Let's validate something for you. Things can be difficult. Life throws some big curveballs at you. But you choose how you will engage with the drama. All the negative, heavy, dark things you're going to experience are very real . . . and it is all part of the excavation process to uncover your innate magic.

## *Be Brave and Boldly Expressive*

You might not believe you're a badass powerful light beam—but know that you really are! You are truly beautiful, vibrant, and fully capable of living bravely in your own power.

You have begun a sacred healing process. Your shadow work will reknit the fragments and lost parts of yourself. This is not something you accomplish and that's it; it's a lifelong journey. Life is a dance between the light and the shadow; it is the contrast that creates the whole of existence.

Go into the world and express yourself. The shadow is born from a lack of love and welcoming for *all* of your parts: the perceived good and bad. As you communicate with your shadow, you will find she is nothing more than the beautiful parts of you that want to be seen and heard. She wants to be real in the world.

Live life as art. How can your life be a form of sacred expression? Here's a little secret: your life is *always* sacred expression. You are a creative force by nature. You just have to get on board with the Universe.

To get on board just ask yourself:

*What holds me back?*

*What am I afraid of?*

*What seems like a big risk?*

*What entices me with excitement and a bit of trepidation?*

*I have never (. . .) because I fear (success, failure, ridicule, etc.)?*

*What feeds your spirit?*

*What makes your heart sing?*

*What gives you joy?*

*What do you close your eyes and dream of doing if "everything" were "perfect"?*

*I feel so light and alive when I (. . .)?*

Declare a radical gesture of self-expression.

Go out into the world . . . *today!* And pick something that feels a little dangerous, but makes your heart sing. Choose something that is completely out of your comfort zone, outside of the walls of what is expected, yet makes you smile inside when you dream of it. Now go do it!

This can be a small or large gesture. It could be ordering a fattening drink at the coffee shop rather than a healthy one. It could be wearing red lipstick to work when you usually don't put on makeup. It could be saying no to your boss/friend/partner even if it means disappointing them. Whatever you do . . . *do it for you!*

You are taking your first steps into creative and spiritual living. The path to healing is the path of self-expression and being in communication with the creative unknown. This is a shamanic journey, a path of alchemical transformation.

You choose how you are going to respond, react, and engage with every single thing in your life.

Don't forget to have boundaries. Boundaries are essential for embracing the shadow, clearing out the mental chatter, and digging into your truth.

Start by say no when you mean *no* and yes when you mean *yes*.

Use your voice. It's the most powerful thing you can do. No one knows how you feel, what you need or want, or what they should do for you if you don't tell them. Communicate your boundaries loud and clear. Whatever opposes your personal truth and well-being is not something you need to give space to in your life.

When you feel dark, when you feel angry, when you feel defeated—use your *voice*. Scream a little. Then speak your truth. Don't shy away from what you want, need, or feel. Those are the most important things in your life; everything else is just filling in the space.

You've got to be a little unconventional to survive. You've got to be audacious enough to show your truth and *thrive*.

Always bring yourself back to center and link in with what you feel. Knowing what hurts shows you how to pivot. And knowing what feels nourishing in your core allows you to stay in the flow.

With each step you take, whether backward or forward, always rock out to this sacred mantra: *"I am a spark of the divine light, magically creating a life of living beauty, color, and sacred expression!"*

# 3

# Going Within

It's too easy to get distracted by world events. Trauma and drama pull us off-center and further away from our own inner wisdom. We're all the walking wounded, doing our best to cope with what's happening out there, often at the price of neglecting what's *inside*. Inner work is necessary if we are going to heal ourselves and show up in the world as whole beings—because *compassion begins within*.

A healthy relationship to self will pave the way for a better relationship with the world, no matter what's happening out there. When we acknowledge our shadow sides and befriend them, we become courageous, merciful. Think about how it would be if everyone did this work! What might the world look like if we were able to forgive and be tender with ourselves?

Introspection is an important step in this shadow work. As we look within, we begin to see those scared, dark spaces, the parts that need our sympathy and love. From there, we can become friends with ourselves, warts and all.

But where do we begin?

## *Try Meditating*

Meditation is one answer.

"Oh, I can't meditate," I hear you saying. Do you think that is true? Many people assume that meditation is hard, that it's for the enlightened few who can sit still for hours, concentrating with a blank mind that even the peskiest fly can't disturb.

Hear this: meditation is not like that—not at all! Meditation is simply sitting still and noticing what comes up. It's a way to practice mindfulness and make peace with the self. While there are formal meditations that require specific breath work or visualization, most practices involve watching the breath. That's it.

But that can require *some* effort. Sitting and observing your breath can be challenging, especially for those who are restless by nature or have difficulty sitting due to physical issues. This is one of the main reasons why so many people attempt a meditation practice only to give it up soon after. So how do you start meditating when the body and mind won't cooperate?

You just start sitting for a few minutes a day. That's all.

Even a five-minute practice will create major transformation. Those few minutes are enough for even the antsiest types to find a quiet space in their day . . . and their mind. Begin doing this and soon you'll see major benefits showing up in every area of your life.

Meditation lowers blood pressure and helps decrease stress. It lessens worry and increases concentration. It promotes healthy digestion and lessens inflammation in the body. Better yet, it helps bring about more mindfulness, and mindfulness is the key to showing up in the world as the best version of yourself.

Face it: a lot of people make decisions or take actions without thinking of the consequences for themselves, other people, or the planet. When did you last think about how your water use when you brush your teeth might impact Mother Earth? If you are mindful, you might think twice before letting that faucet run while you rinse out your mouth. When you post an opinion on someone's social media profile, do you stop to consider how your words, even if well-intentioned, might harm that person? Again, if you're mindful, you might think carefully before clicking send. A mindful attitude promotes peace.

Meditation can create that for you. For anyone who actively participates, meditation is the key to healing the shadow and making the world a better place for us all.

A few tips:

1. Find a quiet place where you will not be disturbed. This may be a room set aside specifically for meditation or a small spot in your bedroom. If you live with other beings, shut the door and put a do not disturb sign on the knob.

2. Make sure the temperature in the room is comfortable. If it's too cold, you will not meditate. You will only focus on how cold you feel. If the room has a chill, be sure to dress in layers and have blankets nearby.
3. Assume a comfortable position. For some, that may mean sitting cross-legged. For others, a chair may be better. Some prefer to lie down on the floor, a couch, or a bed. Others who may have physical conditions may be happier in a wheelchair or seated with cushions and pillows around the body. Find what works for your needs and then settle in.
4. Choose a focal point. You may want to bring your awareness to the rise and fall of your belly or the breath as it comes in and out through the nostrils.
5. Observe your breath without trying to change it or control it. Just let it come and go and watch. If a thought pops into your mind, label the thought and then let it go. For example, if you find yourself starting to plan your dinner menu, as soon as you catch yourself doing that, label it "planning" and then go back to watching your breath. You may end up doing this over and over, but don't fret—you are getting clued in to how your brain likes to operate!
6. Do not judge your practice as "wrong" or "right." It's right for you, as it is. It's totally personal.
7. Sit for as long as you are comfortable. In the beginning, that may only be three minutes. That's fine! Aim for about five minutes a day, but even if that is too hard, give yourself credit for what you *are* able to do!
8. A little journaling after meditation is a wonderful way to wrap up your practice. Keep a journal handy and jot down your observations. It's interesting to revisit those notes later on as your practice matures.

   Here is a simple meditation practice that you may want to try out.

## Loving-Kindness/Metta Meditation

This meditation is ideal when you're feeling sad about the state of the world or dealing with some particularly nasty people. Empathic folk can get easily drained or depleted by a topsy-turvy world or a mean comment. This meditation pulls you back into compassion mode.

Sit comfortably and close your eyes. Begin following your breath. As you inhale silently say to yourself, "May I be free from suffering." On the exhale: "May I be at peace." Repeat this mantra with each breath. Practice for a few minutes.

You can also direct the mantra toward a hater/world event/world leader/negative person in the media, etc., if you find they are pulling you off-center or bringing you down. In this case, you would replace *I* with the name of the difficult person. For example: "May Bob be free from suffering. May Bob be at peace." By sending good energy to this person, you're breaking the negative connection between you. More importantly, you're sending out much-needed healing and compassion. Negative types and situations need that the most.

Remember: Hurt people hurt people. Loving-kindness meditation transforms that.

## *EFT Is Another Option*

You are a growing and expanding microcosmic universe composed of energy. We call this your energetic story where all your experiences, traumas, and beliefs are held. From this energetic story, the narrative of your life is written.

Energy cannot be created or destroyed, as science tells us, so it is always vibrating. That vibration dictates the form it becomes. If you change the vibration, you change the form, and if you change the form, you can change the whole picture of your life.

Look at it this way: If water is the energy we are working with, the vibration will dictate the form that water takes. From a low to high vibration, water becomes ice, liquid, then gas. It's all the same stuff, just a different form based on the vibration. Your energetic story follows the same principle.

If your energy is stuck at the rate of an old trauma or belief, then your life becomes a chronic cycle of similar experiences. When you shift the vibration, you change your life. It's simple in theory but takes a lot more work in practice. That is why intention is so key!

One way to shift your energy and clear out the old trauma that has cluttered up your story is by using EFT, or the Emotional Freedom Technique. EFT is a visceral way of shifting energy. According to *EFT-Alive.com*: "The cause of all negative emotions and beliefs is a disturbance in our body's energy system." So you work with your body and intention to move your blocked energy.

EFT functions on the premise that your body has energetic pathways called meridians that contribute to your well-being or lack thereof. If your energy is flowing smoothly through these meridians, then you are well, but if it is stuck or blocked from some past trauma, then you will experience disease.

When you do EFT, you are tapping into the vibration by acknowledging the block or trauma you experienced. Because energy is not bound by time or space, there is no difference between now and when you first experienced this trauma. You can recall the pain and begin to move it from the past into the here and now, just like you will use the Tarot to look at an old story, see it in full expression, and begin to rewrite it!

Your power to create by feeling is immense. If you can feel something intently, you can activate that vibration throughout your life. You can use your emotions, energy, magic, and intention to create abundance just as easily as you can produce lack. The thing you believe in the most will become the truth. For this reason, it's important to allow what you feel when it arises, be with it, and then let it go. If not, it becomes a seed lodged in your energy where it takes root and blooms into repeated experience.

EFT is one of the many ways you can experience the negative feeling, recall the trauma, and release it with intention rather than chewing on it endlessly! As *EFT-Alive.com* explains, "EFT works by intentionally activating an energy disturbance by thinking about a painful memory or just feeling your feelings. As the disturbance gets cleared through the tapping, you will experience your negative emotions actually drain away."

Not only do the negative emotions dissipate, but their shifting makes space for a new vibration to fill. However you look at it, the intentional shift is the key to creating the change. We cannot speak to the physical benefits of EFT on healing the body and disease, but we have found this technique has tremendous benefits for releasing energies that keep us from experiencing our higher purpose.

## How to Do EFT

Performing an EFT session on yourself is simple. You will call up some trauma, negative experience, or emotion you are grappling with. Then you will go through a series of tapping different places on your body to release the energy to be replaced or transformed.

1. Acknowledge what you are releasing. This can be a very specific trauma, a feeling, or something happening right now. Come up with a clear phrase that encapsulates

this experience. This can be a memory, a present issue, a feeling, etc. Work on one issue at a time! For example: I am lonely, or I hate my job, or my father was never there for me. Unlike affirmations, your statement is focused on the negative. You are trying to conjure up the negative feeling at its fullest so it can be released through the tapping exercise.

2. Rate on a scale of 0–10 how painful the feeling is. We'll use this later to check in on your pain level after a couple of tapping passes. The idea is to tap until there is no pain left.

3. Set up the session by using a phrase that pinpoints the trauma or feeling and accepts it so it can be released. The most common phrase used in EFT is: "Even though (your statement), I deeply and profoundly accept myself." You can change this according to your situation, but this is the classic formula used.

4. Now begin your tapping:

    1. Tap quickly with all stiff fingers on the side of your palm (this can be either hand). Repeat two to three times, "Even though (your statement), I deeply and profoundly accept myself."

    2. Tap on the top of your head with your whole palm quickly, repeating just one time your original statement, without the "even though" piece.

    3. Tap the inside point of your eyebrow on either side near your nose, repeating just your statement once.

    4. Tap the outside point of your eye (either eye), repeating just your statement once.

    5. Tap under your eye bone close to your nose, repeating just your statement once.

    6. Tap the space between your nose and lips, repeating just your statement once.

    7. Tap your chin, repeating just your statement once.

    8. Tap the point of your collarbone on one side, repeating just your statement once.

9. Tap under your armpit a few inches down (either side) with an open palm, repeating just your statement once.
10. Gently tap your wrists together and repeat, "Even though (your statement), I deeply and profoundly love, accept, and forgive myself."
11. Go through the series one more time.

5. Now that you've moved through the tapping sequence twice, assess the intensity level of your feeling. If you are down to 1 or 0, then you can stop. If you still feel triggered, go through the series again. This time you can rework your original statement to reflect the changes you feel. For example: I still feel lonely, or my job is still unbearable.
6. Finally, go through the tapping series one more time, but change the statement to a positive affirmation. An example might be "I am confident with who I am and I deeply and profoundly love, accept, and forgive myself."

You can go through the EFT sequence for any issue whenever you need it. I (Shaheen) find it really helpful when I am in the midst of something and I need to work through it. Just going to the bathroom for a few minutes to tap it out can shift everything quickly!

There are many wonderful resources for EFT practices on the web, but this is the basic recipe that most practitioners follow. You will find slight variations depending on the source. Online videos can help you see the process if you are a more visual person. To learn more, check out *EFT-Alive.com* and *thetappingsolution.com*.

## *Other Ways to Connect with Yourself and the World*

### Shine Your Light and Magic in the Face of Adversity

Shaheen has always lived his life on the edge of dreamland as a little free-spirited soul dancing between what is seen and what isn't:

"There is magic all around us, rooted deep within. Most of us fear its innate power. But my magic has always been alive within me, seeking expression and wanting to be shared with the world.

My favorite ritual is to go out into the thick of night, under a bright, full moon, and spin. I spin with passion, I spin with grace. My gossamer wings taking flight in the light, transcending the physical and moving into something deeply mystical—a little white witch fed by lunar fire.

## Life Exists in Two Worlds

There is the world of rational thought, the world you can touch, which everyone inhabits. Most of us know this world far too well, to the point of feeling stuck in place, heavy with gravity, and weighed down with reality.

Then there is the ephemeral world. This world lies within. It's a dream world where anything is possible, a forgotten territory where magic is alive and well. This is the world of the creative, the artist—a world of living poetry.

Most of us long for this place, although few of us ever acknowledge it, but the door is always there, waiting to be opened. The door is nothing outside of you; it lies on the path of your inner world, your sacred circle of truth, magic, and spirit.

Empowerment comes when you learn to be in both worlds. It's like walking on the edge of the water, half in the ocean and half on land. The 'tween places are where anything is possible. Vision and reality become one . . . infused with divine grace and potential.

## Sacred Space Can Change Your Life

Do you want to experience a powerful form of *personal transformation*? Creating sacred space is an act of being present in the here and now. *When you create sacred space, you are giving yourself permission to release negative patterns and consciously set seeds of intention for change.*

And anyone can create sacred space. When you take the time to do so, you are acknowledging the life force that lives inside of you. On a deep level, you are feeding an intrinsic need for stillness and touching the mystical.

### CRAFTING CEREMONY

Ceremony is at the core of all spiritual traditions and creates a psychological shift that quiets the analytical mind and awakens the intuitive. In moments of stillness, you are stepping outside of time, *surrendering to your inner wisdom*, and affirming that you need and want to nurture your highest good.

The world is a fast-paced, high-energy environment that overwhelms the senses, and much of the time, it shuts down our necessary connection to our deeper self. You can see this in the drama on the news, the depression that permeates our society, and the lack of openness we experience in daily life.

Pain points, whether in our personal lives or our society, are the result of a lack of love. *Love comes only when we are open, fluid, and willing to accept and forgive.* These are the qualities that come from being in communion with your spirit and working toward your highest good.

To reach for this state of well-being and expressions of love, *we must create sacred time*. Here you ignite your intuition, feed your spirit, and become truly empowered. Learning this dance ripples outward, changing the people and situations around you.

## FIRST CREATE SACRED TIME

Close your eyes for a second. Take a few deep, cleansing breaths—in and out. Find your rhythm. Feel your center. Feel your sitting bones pushing into the earth beneath you. Feel your skeleton sustaining you. Feel yourself in this moment, now.

*What does it look like inside?*

*What does it feel like?*

*What word would you use to describe this moment right now?*

Maybe this process overwhelms you. Maybe you have taken little time to be still. There is no guilt. Everyone at some point forgets to nurture the spiritual self. But this is a call to action. We are setting an intention to go inward.

## NOW LET'S CREATE SACRED SPACE

Do you want to create sacred space and inspire this internal shift?

We're sure you do. Everyone yearns for this. Let's begin now. This decision affords you an opportunity to change—and create. Make the life you want, the healing you need, and the empowerment you seek.

Sacred space is a physical and an internal place.

If you look at the world around you, most importantly your home, you will find that this is a reflection of your inner world. This can be an overwhelming idea, but it is a point of power.

*What does your outer world look like?*

*What state is your home in?*

*What does the state of your home say about the state of your life?*

Pick one area of your home to transform.

Begin with your bedroom, where you sleep and where you retreat from the world. Pick up the pile of clothes in the corner. Organize the books and papers next to the bed. Clear out the clutter from under the bed. Wash and replace the sheets. Add something new to the environment that inspires a feeling of peace, relaxation, and vitality.

As you move forward with this process, be gentle. Take baby steps. You may need to do one room at a time or face one issue at a time. Go forth with an intention of healing, connecting to your highest good, and eliciting positive change.

Affirm your intentions: *I am at peace clearing away the clutter, connecting with my inner light, and creating my sacred space.*

Now that you have begun to shift the external world, the inner world will change too. This is a process of purging. Affirm what you want and don't want in your life. Graciously and fluidly let things go. You are welcoming new energy.

Doesn't it feel good to invite new energy into your life?

Focus on other areas of your home. Look around your home. Look for a corner, a room, or a little nook that you can make into your spiritual haven. This will be your place of power. Here you will cultivate your sacred space to go inward.

Pinpoint this area and envision how you can make this a place of power. Add color. Place a chair, pillow, or blanket that makes you feel safe and comforted. Gather together anything that has energetic value.

Items of energetic value can be inspiring photos—images of mentors, spiritual guides, and loved ones. Place statues of the Divine in your space. Set crystals here for high vibration. Keep a fresh candle in your sacred space to light as a reminder that this is a place of power to ignite your highest good.

## NOW USE YOUR SACRED SPACE

Make daily time in your space. Meditate, pray, and set intentions for change here. Now revisit the meditation above, closing your eyes and going inward. Answer those questions once again.

You will see a difference. Every sacred moment raises your vibration, claiming your space in the world, the Universe, and your spirit. Work to say no to negative thoughts and lovingly replace them with something better.

One last power thought. In each thing that you do, ask yourself:

*Does this feed my spirit or does it deplete my spirit?*

## Everything Is Made of Energy

You are a vibrating, microcosmic Universe. You are a multifaceted being made of energy and intention. You are not just your body; you are a corona of light and frequency. Some call this the aura—the rainbow layers of color that surround you. We call this your energetic story!

Your energetic story is composed of your thoughts, ideas, and beliefs about the world and how you fit into it. On this energetic level, you are pushing and pulling things into your life, interacting with the people and places around you.

Everything begins on the energetic level: the state of your health and the state of your life, as well as the people and situations that surround you. Everything is an out-picturing of your inner world. Energy is like currency: you invest in and feed whatever you place your attention on.

Most of us live our lives unaware of this powerful spiritual truth. Once you begin to understand that you are energy, you can begin to shift your focus and consciously manifest the life you want!

### OVERCOMING ANXIETY, EMPOWERING YOUR THOUGHTS, AND CLEARING AWAY ENERGETIC BONDS

Shaheen sometimes finds himself being swept away in the storm:

"I am a little paper boat, carried away by the wind and the rain. In the chaos of the thrashing, torrential waters, I feel my spirit call out, only to be deafened by anxiety and frustration. As fear builds, I sink deeper into despair, descending down and down . . . farther away from the wisdom of my spirit and into the muddy waters of lack and separation.

A storm of energy rages through the atmosphere around us. The malignant creation of our negative thought forms and feelings floats in and out of our heads and hearts. This is a natural by-product of our negative self-talk, our daily discontent, frustration, and the occasional ill will we "harmlessly" project onto others. These energies are dust accumulating on and around us—energetic toxins.

That's not to say there is no good energy and intention out there. But they just add to our vibrancy and vitality. What we are concerned with are the negative or stray energies that whirl around us, clouding our spiritual receptors and tainting our energetic story. It's as if we are trying to paint the masterpiece of our lives with a dirty paintbrush.

The spite from an angry driver on the way to work, the unhappy barista making your latte, the melancholy rider next to you on the train—all are projecting unbridled energetic toxins and clutter through the atmosphere. It's a natural part of living, like dust or trash, and goes mostly unnoticed, but after enough collects, you become heavy, vulnerable, and even ill.

No one is to blame, yet we are all responsible. Let's do our part to keep the psychic atmosphere clean and to raise our vibration in the process. It feels good to be happy and whole. Plus, it is one step closer to living life more abundantly!

When you find yourself enmeshed in a web of limiting beliefs, past issues, and confusion, moving forward can seem like hell. But how do you find composure? Releasing the past so that the future can come forward, clean and clear, is something we all want and need . . . at least once in our lives. Personally, these situations creep up on us. Before we know it, we are tangled up with no end in sight.

## Basic Human Nature

Our experience in these moments is basic human nature. We all feel this heavy weight of unknowing and lack mentality. When things knock us off course, we seem to give in to the frustration and lose our sense of self and, most notably, our deepest intention to thrive and grow.

The secret lives in the eye of the storm—that gentle feeling of closing your eyes and moving into the rhythm of the moment. In this place at the center of chaos lives the flow—the flow of life, abundance, and prosperity. One thing always holds true: you can change your reaction, regardless of the nature of your situation. And you can use negative situations for good too.

## Finding Strength on the Path of Understanding

Shaheen shares this story about strength:

"I sat in a room with a longtime friend and client, surrounded by gilded mirrors, beautiful china teacups, and luscious fabrics. Her face was bright, open, and inviting. I sipped tea and listened as she spoke. I listened to her words and her heart. Something was brewing deep inside her.

Finally she said, "I am outraged. I am outraged by how I was treated. I put my life into my work, and yet I feel disrespected, as if nothing I did really mattered. This isn't how retirement should feel. I wanted to leave with grace, knowing I left behind something that would grow into the future."

Her intensity surprised me. The fire in her belly didn't match her serene demeanor. Yet I could feel the truth in every word she spoke. She wanted to know that her energy wasn't wasted. Her inner world and her outer world weren't aligned. There was a crinkle in her story, the story of her truth, and the story of those around her.

Then she leapt into another concern about her community. An injustice had taken place, jeopardizing the integrity of the people in a very respected neighborhood. This place that had been built on dream and good intentions was being torn apart by greed and underhanded dealings. And she wanted justice!

She openly asked, "What should I do?"

Knowing that both her outrage about her retirement and the state of her community were linked together, I decide to pull a card for advice on how best to use her energy.

You see, this is a woman who is passionate and altruistic. She dreams the big dream, the dream of the community and the well-being of those around her. She can see the big picture.

I pulled one card: Strength.

The Strength card in the Tarot portrays a serene woman with her hand in the mouth of a mighty lion. Unfazed and unafraid of the raw force and power of this awesome creature, she subdues the lion through empathy rather than force, knowing and acknowledging that she is like the lion himself: a wild-hearted creature pulled and enlivened by her deepest nature.

I began to relay her message . . .

"As you set out on a path to live unencumbered by the weight of daily living, you hold space where power can gather. Rather than fight the world, you begin to move through it, dancing within the eye of this great storm, because the world will continue to rage around you. You cannot escape the world by retreating inward. Eventually you will suffocate. Reach out and touch the raw force of nature, the spiral of chaos. Use this as your medium to paint something more like your own internal vision."

Strength was reminding her that it wasn't enough to feel outraged. She needed to use this energy for something. A solution wouldn't come from being hurt. It wouldn't come from sitting in meetings. Rather, change would happen when she began to live her truth.

Days later, the Strength card kept appearing in sessions, her energy wanting to come alive and express to us her deepest meaning. I began to really meditate on her meaning.

What message did she have to teach?

Her message was loud and clear: I know that fire too, the fire my client felt. It's the fire we all feel when our internal vision and the external world no longer dance together. Isn't that usually the case?

## You Are a Visionary Being Called to Action

If you are reading this, it means you are one of the visionaries in the world. And you are called to action and drawn to the path of self-discovery. Through self-discovery comes expression, and from expression comes change in the big world. As you follow your inner vision in the outer world, you create change through empathy rather than force.

The art of magic is the process of creating miracles through natural force. In all spiritual traditions, we find ways to touch the Divine through the material. You can't negate the physical to find the ephemeral; it is through the physical that you touch magic.

Contemplate your own body for a moment. What a beautiful force of nature it is. It holds and sustains you. You are your body, and yet you live beyond it. We talk in terms of dreams, goals, and the hypothetical. Those things do not exist anywhere in a physical sense, but it is through the physical that we can speak about them, express them, and begin to create them!

How many times have you sat in a room lit with aromatic candles and felt transformed? Candles are nothing more than wax and fire. They are physical creations. But simply lighting a candle for relaxation, ambience, or prayer allows us to transcend time and space. It speaks to the mystical mind in an inexplicable way.

The point we are trying to make is that by being in the external world, you actually build a path to the internal. Or working through the inner world, you see changes in the outer. Find the magic in everyday life. Then you will create more magic.

The blocked spots, the pain, the setbacks, the adversity in your life are a call to action. If you just observe the stuck spots in your life and the world at large, then you are not creating change. There is no room for apathy in magical living. Let these blocks become oracles showing you a point of power to make changes.

There is an old saying: as above, so below. Any changes you make in the inner world shift the external. Many great spiritual leaders have guided us to be the change we wish to see in the world. Actions speak louder than words!

## Create Change through Empathy, Not Force

Create change through empathy, not force. Whatever calls your attention is a message from your intuition saying, "Hey, you can do something about this . . . big or small!"

The world needs us to return to self-care consciousness.

You are unique, dramatic, beautiful, and magic. You are made of the light of the Universe, the dust of the stars. The moon lives in the lining of your skin and the glow in your eyes. Give it to the world.

Ask yourself:

*How am I expressing myself in the world?*

*Am I telling my truth?*

*Where am I losing my power?*

If you are holding your head down and avoiding eye contact with what is happening around you, then you are forgetting your magic. You came here to be magic! Be empathetic with yourself. That self-care will pour out into the world around you.

Honoring yourself is a sacred act of rebellion. The world doesn't always take kindly to those who choose an alternative route. Raging against the collective consciousness of what is right, proper, and responsible can throw up a lot of obstacles. But this wild-hearted approach to living is what activates your magic and self-expression.

There are times we find ourselves crushed under the weight of what we *should* do, rather than trusting what we feel *called* to do. But when we go deeper inside, we realize honoring the call of our inner wisdom is actually the path to wholeness. Well-meaning people protest when we try to take this approach because they are uncomfortable with owning their own power.

## Learning to Go with the Flow

Swimming in the storm becomes harder when you lose composure and give in to fear. You cannot anticipate what is next, so rather than fighting, flailing around, and sinking, be with it. Hold space for the experience and see where it might take you. Sometimes these trying moments are actually the upheaval of energy pushing you into the next phase, the next chapter of your story.

Reaching into this overwhelming sense of darkness often rewards us with beautiful treasures. Move into the storm of transformation, and you will find a new groove. What you initially experience as chaos is usually a wake-up call. Your spirit and the Universe have partnered together to ask the big questions:

*Do you know what you are intending to do?*

*What are you feeling versus what you are wanting to feel?*

*How are you taking care of yourself?*

When things aren't working, we may actually be moving against our own flow. We are going against the grain. Rather than pushing harder, it becomes easier to sit down and take stock of what is happening and why. Maybe Spirit is moving you to an easier path. Maybe this isn't the path to go down at the moment. Or maybe you need to move a little slower, taking in the sights around you.

## Move into the Storm

Try not to have tunnel vision in these moments of chaos. Be with the experience, rather than the desired outcome. Be in this moment and see what is bubbling to the surface. These are the gifts of the shadow, our unacknowledged dark parts where our potential lives.

Make no definitive decisions in this turbulent place, because these cracks in your awareness will soon become fertile space for new seeds to grow. The secret of stepping into your personal flow lies in your ability to accept and experience whatever lies before you. Trying, visceral experiences often shake us up to purge away the psychic debris and challenge us on what we really want, need, intend, and believe to be true!

We like to move into the storm, wrap ourselves in the water, and compassionately ask:

*What do I have left to learn here?*

*How can I honor my highest good?*

Breathing into the chaos, the darkness, and asking these questions lead us to growing calmer, clearer, and more able to move with the storm. The skies begin to brighten, and the world becomes more serene. Our uncertainty and anxiety have magnified the storm, because the Universe is a big mirror.

We psyche ourselves out. A challenge appears, and we move into fight or flight. In every situation, regardless of what the next move might be, find your footing. Take in the atmosphere around you. That is the only way to thrive in trying times.

## Releasing Chatter and Honoring Your Truth

Finding composure usually begins with stillness. Knots of anxiety cannot tighten if you stop flailing around for dear life. Composure comes in these moments of intentional silence. Taking time will unwind your thoughts and mental chatter, which tend to breed anxiety and fear. We need to relieve the internal pressure, so our hearts can guide us to clarity!

When you find yourself fraught with anxiety and tension, become still. Do this by walking in nature. Your soul will be nourished and your mind detoxified. You might engage in some breath work or use a guided meditation. Stillness pulls you from the past, where anxiety multiplies, and into the present where clarity can take root.

Seek out your inner truth. Sometimes that can feel lonely, isolating, and draining. When you find yourself feeling the strain of living your truth, you are actually going through a psychic detox. You are releasing the old, worn-out patterns that have existed for longer than you can imagine. If you act from your wisest self, you will find you are on a unique path of radical self-expression.

Be honest with yourself by looking for the black holes in your life.

*What is sucking away your energy?*

*What are you tied to that doesn't honor your spirit?*

*What is old and worn-out?*

*Can you purge some of these attachments?*

Whether these black holes are people, things, responsibilities, or beliefs, you can begin to let go. Usually they are a combination of all the above. Because our inner world is mirrored back to us through our outer life, these things can be very revealing. Try giving away what no longer tells your story. Say goodbye to people who no longer empower your spirit, and say no to things that only make you feel unhappy.

Your life is your prayer. Whatever you choose to do should honor and expand your soul. The path may not always be clear, but the calling will be strong when you listen to it. Cultivate a practice of going inward and hearing the chatter in your head and the stirring in your heart.

Does your inner voice sound like fear?

If you are met with fear, then you are not leading from your wisest self. Rather, you are reacting to your truth and feeling the strain of the collective consciousness around you. Delve deeper and slip further into your body and soul until you find your longing.

*What do you long for?*

*What do you dream of?*

*What makes you feel alive (when you forgo analyzing if it is right or wrong, good or bad)?*

## The Purest Moments . . .

These moments of pure, be-here-now presence are what dreams are made of it. Whether you are in the present moment feeling happy or sad, fearful or accepting, when you are truly in the now you are gathering power and finding clarity. Yet most of us spend our time scattered across different lives, different continents, and different periods in time until we are nothing but a storm of diffused fragments that cannot find any traction.

Fear keeps most of us from even momentarily being present because we might discover something that we didn't want to acknowledge. We might have to get real about what isn't working. How funny is it that we want answers and change, but we don't want to do the hard work? Perspective is everything in the present. You could see these revelations and clarity as painful reminders of your soft spots and vulnerabilities, or you can see them as they really are—opportunities for big magic!

## What Being Present Means

When Shaheen slips into his own darkness—be it sadness, fear, anger, or angst—he knows he has cut himself off from the flow of the Universe and, more specifically, the present moment. Now, being in the present moment isn't about being oblivious to the past or the future or even the things going on in the world and your life as a whole. Being in the present moment is about not being attached to the chaos and giving away your power.

You can observe the scene unfolding without interacting. It's sort of like when your parents told you to look but not touch. Choose wisely and intently the things you wish to place your hands and heart upon. That way, you are in full agreement about where that road could take you. Then you lay your spirit upon that intention and fall curious to what comes next.

Being present is about letting go of the need to control. When you want to control the outcome over everything, rather than focusing on the task at hand, you are slipping out of the present! Surrendering to the circle of intention that is the "right now" is a powerful gesture. You relinquish your need to do a million things at one time while getting nowhere fast. Imagine a life of just flowing rather than forcing!

## Be Here Now

Simply call yourself back to the present throughout the day. Pull yourself back into the hum of the room, the solid earth beneath you, and the rhythm of your own breathing. You become present, grounded in the here and now, which is where the flow of intention flourishes. It is a simple, sacred act of fortifying the spirit.

## Breath Connects You to Life and Life Is in the Present Moment

Breath work is a simple way to bring yourself into the present. We push our bodies way too hard, taking for granted good food, good sleep, and, most importantly, healthy breathing. Shallow breaths create stagnant and scattered energy and intentions. As you move into the cycles of your breathing with intention, you rejuvenate your body, clear your mind, process your emotional centers, and ground yourself in the here and now.

Breathing is healing in these moments. Your breath connects you to your body, to your spirit, and allows you to be present. Presence is the key to wellness. If you slip out of your body in the face of uncertainty, then you lose your grounding and your ability to communicate with your spirit.

Affirm to yourself: *I am here now, in this moment, in this experience, ready for the ride.*

The challenge of being in the moment is ever present. Being present isn't being idle; it is being aware of what is happening at this moment now. Shaheen says "When I feel chaotic, I usually allow myself to have a freak-out, and then I stop and remind myself that there is something to learn here."

### SIMPLE BREATH WORK TO MOVE YOU INTO THE PRESENT

1. Activate your breathing session by getting comfortable. Let yourself become settled wherever you are: in your chair, on a bench, beneath a tall tree, at your desk, or in your bed. Loosen your shoulders by swinging your arms gently. Shake out your limbs. Release the muscles in your face. Feel yourself sinking deeper into the ground beneath you, into the moment, and into your breathing.

2. Sip cool, refreshing air through your nose. Pull your breath deep into your belly, feeling it grow and expand. Now let your middle expand and then your chest. Once you are full, begin to exhale through your mouth.

3. As you exhale, feel a stair-step rhythm begin to happen. Release your breath from the chest first, then the middle, then the belly. Reverse the order as you inhale through the nose again.

4. Feel yourself building energy as your breathing takes on a flowing rotation: inhale . . . exhale . . . inhale . . . exhale. The ebb and flow of your breathing will activate your body's natural flow, moving energy blocks, bringing you into the present moment, and granting you wisdom and knowledge stored deep within.

5. Try this exercise for at least five minutes, or go as long as you need. Your whole body will relax and return to a state of wellness. Your stress levels will decrease, and you will begin to see the masterpiece of your life unfolding before you.

## OTHER TIPS TO GROUND YOURSELF IN THE MOMENT

Stretching and body movement such as walking, yoga, or swimming will connect you with your body. Feeling our body helps us to be more present because we tend to slip outside of it when things become difficult. Or mindfully enjoy a cup of warm herbal tea or a light snack. The EFT Tapping we explored earlier is another amazing technique for releasing and becoming present.

Try noticing what is around you when you are feeling out of touch or spacey. Like playing Where's Waldo, begin mindfully taking in the space you are occupying. Find three colors in your current setting. Find three shapes. Find three different sounds. Find three different smells. Find three different textures you can touch. Look up, down, and side to side.

When you are feeling off-kilter, questioning your thoughts is another practice to use. Begin by noticing your thoughts. Write them down on a piece of paper or speak them out loud to a recorder. I like to do this in a mirror, so I can see the truth in my eyes. Go deep and get to the heart of what is happening in your mind.

Then simply ask yourself:

*Is this thought true?*

*Do I have proof?*

*What is the worst that can happen?*

*What if it is all a lie?*

*What if it is nothing more than fear?*

*What can I do to actively change it right now?*

*Can I name this thought or find its source?*

Do this whenever you are met with anxious feelings. One time could feel like a fall down the rabbit hole. However, with time, pulling your thoughts out of your head and questioning them will reveal the content of your mind, how it is really narrating your life, and how limiting it truly is. Far too often, we spend our time telling ourselves very scary things that do nothing but disrupt our internal state and throw everything into chaos. It doesn't have to be that way. This practice will help you cultivate intentional living.

## Be Nowhere

When Shaheen needs major healing and clarity, he likes to slip out of the time loop of daily life. This is an intuitive approach to becoming neutral. Removing yourself from the situation abolishes the limiting patterns and tunnel vision that can sometimes bleed us of our insight. It's like walking away from a frustrating problem to then be met with a sudden solution.

Sleeping is the number one way that you can go neutral. When you need answers, sleep on it. When you sleep, you move yourself into the receptive mode of being. You release tension and the need to control. You move into sacred time where you are nourished by divine light and spiritual guidance. Sleep is the act of plugging in your spiritual battery to recharge.

Meditation and trance are more intentional ways of moving into the neutral, "nowhere" state. You are quieting the analytical self to allow the intuitive self to step forward. Embarking on this sacred journey of transformation awakens an innate desire to be in your spirit. Shamanic rattling and drumming can enhance meditation/trance work. The drum and rattle help to subdue the analytical mind, so the spirit self can speak. Ten to fifteen minutes a few times a week can be a wonderful place to begin.

## A Way of Life

Spiritual cleansing is psychic detoxification. It is purging and clearing out the aura. Spiritual hygiene aligns you to your highest good, your innate wisdom. Claiming energetic space activates magnetism to make magic happen!

Your mental/emotional state is a big player in your energetic storytelling. Thoughts and feelings are active, living forces that work to push, pull, and clarify whatever you are bringing into your life. Negative thoughts and feelings have a lower frequency, causing disturbances in your aura, weakening your protection, and inviting unwanted influence.

Emotions color and clarify thoughts. What you feel evokes what you think. As you accept limiting thoughts, you invite more feelings, creating a cycle that is all too real and very damaging.

Thankfully, we have the power to disrupt this cycle. Not every negative thought or feeling will instantly show up in your life. But it's like when you consistently ingest unhealthy food and your health begins to suffer. So one negative thought won't be damaging, just as one positive thought won't be healing. It is through habit that we cultivate good energetic hygiene.

## Claim Your Space

Claiming your space is taking ownership of what you will and will not accept in your life. By fortifying your energy bodies, you keep negative energies at bay and attract more of the good that you wish for. Like frequencies of a radio, whatever rate you vibrate at allows you to tap into anything at that frequency.

Staying mentally and emotionally alert declares your space. Essentially you are saying, "Where I am right now—is this where I want to be?" This state of being is what we call your "personal bubble." You are building a Universe based on what feels good to you!

Try to recall someone you've met who seems to radiate a personal force field. They have a seemingly impenetrable bubble of protection that keeps you treading just around the perimeter comfortably out of their space!

These individuals have made energetic space for their own well-being. Though they may seem intimidating, introverted, unapproachable, or even arrogant, they often are none of those things. Rather they have made an effort to cultivate their well-being by protecting their spirit self and their thoughts and feelings.

Declare your own space by staying mentally and emotionally alert. Stay accountable for your state of being and make a daily effort to check in with yourself to measure where you are and what you are projecting out into the ether.

This projection is what those around you are swimming through, and interacting and responding to accordingly.

Turn your attention to what you are thinking and feeling. It may feel unnatural at first to filter your thoughts and feelings, but after a while it will become second nature. You will never be immune to negative thinking, or down feelings, but you will begin to sense a shift in your state of well-being as you go there and can consciously shift out!

This state of awareness allows you to clarify what you are projecting outward into the ether and refine how and in what way people will respond to and interact with you. Oh, and it's okay to be a little tough sometimes or to seem a little standoffish. An element of mystery never hurt anyone.

You'll find this very helpful when you are among large groups of people, in tense situations, or feeling under pressure from work. Turning inward in this way may seem a little redundant or unnecessary, but we promise, you will be surprised at how unaware of your present state of being you usually are.

We know we are often the last to know how we really feel or what we are really thinking until we make the effort to pay attention. We are constantly catching negative thoughts by the tail as they float out of our mind, declaring "you're thinking it again" and making an effort to shift. Sometimes even talking out loud to others in this way can be helpful. Be honest about where you are!

As you create the space and cultivate the practice of noticing your thoughts and feelings, you can replace them with something more wholesome and uplifting, essentially nullifying your shadowy state.

Ask yourself this very profound question again:

*Does this feed my spirit or does it deplete my spirit?*

Ask this question in any given situation. You'll begin to see the patterns of what builds you up or tears you down. Break the cycle of what is limiting, and you banish its power. We know this is easier said than done. But it is the basic truth of spiritual cleansing and protection.

**FOUR WAYS TO CLAIM YOUR SPACE**

1. Take daily stock of where you are mentally and emotionally.
2. Spend time in prayer and meditation to consciously shift into a high vibration.
3. Ground and center in moments of chaos. Simply stepping outside to wrap your arms around a tree will ground you. You can also work on your breathing, allowing yourself to find the rhythm of your breath. Visualize yourself rooting into the earth like a tree. This will discharge unwanted energies.
4. Create sacred space. This can be a formal process of making a spiritual haven for connecting with the Divine or simply generating an environment or atmosphere that makes you feel good.

## Exercise to Shift Your Energetic State

Begin making a daily practice of observing your thoughts. Your thoughts are the way you process and shift your emotions. Throughout the day—especially in those hectic times when you tend to lose track of yourself—consciously stop and ask yourself:

*What am I thinking right now?*

*What am I feeling right now?*

*What is driving these feelings and these thoughts?*

When you catch yourself at the tail end of a limiting thought, swap it out with a more uplifting one. For every negative thought you have, replace it with three positive ones. Activate these three positive thoughts by affirming them out loud.

For example: Say you are thinking of your shortcomings and weaknesses on a project you are doing for work. Nullify that limiting pattern by affirming out loud, or in your head:

*(Your negative thought) may not be my strong point, but I am EXCELLENT at (positive thought 1), (positive thought 2), and (positive thought 3). I have this under control and it's flowing smoothly!*

Begin to imagine that affirmation playing out in your head. Go through the story in your head. See yourself really embodying those three positive attributes. As you envision these attributes, you activate your feelings, raising your vibration and shifting your energetic story.

Check in again, asking:

*What am I feeling right now?*

*What am I projecting outward into the world with my emotions?*

Another fun question to ask is:

*What color am I right now?*

Just close your eyes and see a color. Do not think too hard about it. Do not think about what color you want to be. Just call out the first color that fills your head. Now you can explore what emotion your color elicits. This is a way of tricking your mind into being honest about your feelings.

End these sessions with a smile. Smiles always make things better. They remind your body to feel good!

As you clarify your emotions through acknowledging your thoughts, you detoxify the psychic atmosphere around you. Refining and redirecting your energy to uplift and support you helps you and everyone in your life.

## *Energetic Cords*

Woven into the fabric of your personal energy field—or bubble as we so often call it—are many fibers, threads, and, most important, cords of energy. Energetic cords are lines of connection between you and another manifestation of energy. We connect ourselves to people, places, objects, and even beliefs and ideas.

### Energy as Currency

When working with energetic cords, we want to identify attachments that deplete our energy. Your energy is your currency with the Universe. You attach to and invest in anything that you hold a strong emotion for. That's not to say that daily, mundane things don't yield energetic cords, but these things don't tend to "stick."

## How Do Negative Energetic Cords Hurt You?

Negative energetic cords are those that essentially deplete your energy. When you attach to something or allow something to attach to you that is not in your best interest, it will drain your vitality. Most of the time this is happening unconsciously, but with a little dedication you can begin to perceive these connections.

Please, do not let this make you feel guilty. We are all multidimensional beings, and we cannot possibly keep up with every facet of our existence. We can only work to be as aware as possible. This is what dictates our energetic story! Your energetic story is a culmination of your thoughts, ideas, and feelings about how you fit into the world and how the world responds to you.

## Signs of Negative Energetic Cords

- Suddenly or chronically feeling tired, drained, or fatigued
- Insomnia
- Sudden bursts of anger
- Altercations and conflicts
- Miscommunications
- Physical pain in the body
- Depression
- Anxiety
- Blocks in key areas of your life
- Feeling off-kilter

Energetic cords can exist for years; others are created and destroyed moment to moment. Anytime you are making an energetic exchange, you are forming an energetic cord. Simply put, this is the mechanics of energy transfer. Energetic cords are pipelines for communicating back and forth. Cords become negative only when they have outlived their purpose.

## How Do Energetic Cords Form?

Imagine opening your front door to welcome a guest and then never securely closing it. After a while, all sorts of things will begin to wander in and out. Before you know it, you will have a guest who has overstayed their welcome and tainted your original hospitality.

These types of exchanges are happening daily, in most situations, with most people. You are allowing cords to form, and you are forming cords with other people. The action of connecting energetically is neutral, but the intention is what pushes it from negative to positive.

In every moment, you want to feel fluid. When you become stuck, rigid, and unaware, you lose the necessary connection to your energy bodies and your deeper self. This results in energetic blocks, negative cords, and overall depletion.

## Becoming Aware of Your Energetic Cords

Often you will find a negative cord is forming when you suddenly feel "off." Or a cord is being "fed" when you're suddenly in a funk or thinking about or fixating on something. At this moment, you need to become aware of your energy. Pay attention to where you are mentally, emotionally, and spiritually.

Bringing your awareness to these three areas will allow you to take ownership of your energy. Begin and end each day by scanning your body. Sense where you are in yourself. Feel your flow of energy. Ask yourself:

*Am I feeding my spirit?*

*Am I depleting my spirit?*

*Am I being fluid?*

*Am I in the past, the present, or the future?*

*Am I fixated on a person, place, thing, or idea?*

*Am I in pain?*

*Where is my pain located?*

*What does my pain look like, feel like, sound like?*

Remember that these energetic cords are ways of communicating and sharing energy with the world around you. This is your energetic investment and exchange. You are trading your spiritual currency with whatever or whomever you have chosen to link it to. In doing this you are either empowering or disempowering yourself.

## Cleaning and Clearing Your Energy

It is essential to ground and center daily. This is especially helpful in high-stress situations or when you are really engrossed in something. Being with people always creates opportunities for energy exchange. When you are in an uninviting place, your essence becomes muddled.

So we go back to inner awareness. We question where we are. Then we take ownership of our energy. Ground yourself in the present moment. Ground yourself into the earth. And center yourself on your present intention.

When you remove an energetic cord, you must also remove the source. If you remove the cord but not the cause, then it will form again. Usually negative cords exist between things that feed our fears and insecurities. Abusive relationships in all their forms are prime contributors to energetic cords. They create a codependency where both parties are feeding off one another energetically. Parasitic ecosystems come to mind.

Removing the source of an energetic cord happens by:

- Being honest.
- Pinpointing the source.
- Naming the emotion/exchange/situation.
- Releasing the want, need, or allowance for the attachment.
- Forgiving everyone involved, as much as possible.
- Sealing and protecting your energy body.

Releasing and removing energetic cords can take time. It is a process that you should repeat daily. Always check in with yourself. Whenever the dynamic of a relationship changes, pay attention to see what energy is connected with that exchange. Time and distance do not matter with cords. So always reaffirm where you are now.

## Tips for Releasing Energetic Cords

Run your hands through your energy bodies to see what you feel. Scanning your aura through your mind's eye is also helpful. I tend to run a selenite wand through my aura as a way of tuning in to its texture and consistency.

If you can, pinpoint the cord. Visualize what the cord looks like. Try to imagine or feel the cord's location, consistency, and purpose.

*Is it thick or thin?*

*Is it rigid, elastic, spongy, or wiry?*

*Does it appear as a certain color?*

*Where is it located?*

*Does it have an image held in it?*

*Why does it exist?*

Energetic cords are pipelines; they hold energies, which carry images and memories. Visualizing the cord can give you clues as to whom or what it is connected to. Sometimes just asking Spirit "what is the source of the attachment?" will give you answers.

Talk out loud to the person or thing the cord is connected to. Just say in your own time and sacred space what you need to say to release this cord. The truth is most cords exist because we have not acknowledged our relationship or connection to something.

Getting it out in the open is the only sure way to release the attachment. Sometimes writing to the source of your energetic cord can offer a chance to acknowledge, forgive, and unplug. Journal about where you are in your life.

Drawing attention and creating awareness about the state of your life give you power. Energetically speaking, you are creating your reality on some level, or at least your relationship to it. You want to consciously manifest the life you want. Mental/emotional work shines light into these areas and empowers you.

You may also want to try the following meditation.

## CORD-CUTTING MEDITATION

Energetically we are constantly giving and receiving energy. When you make a connection, it is charged with energy that creates an energetic cord. An energetic cord is a vibrational communication line. Cords often outlive their usefulness, leading to energy drain, mood swings, negative thoughts, and overall depletion. Cutting cords calls back your energy so you can regain equilibrium.

Find a relaxed position. Inhale deep into your belly. Fill yourself with beautiful white light. Exhale all tension. Inhale, feeling your belly rise, and exhale, feeling your belly fall. Like a wave washing over you, you will begin to find your rhythm.

Gently scan your body. Become aware of areas in your body that feel "off," heavy, painful, or tingly. Trust whatever you feel. Notice what impressions appear. This is an energetic cord no longer serving your highest good. Perceive the cord in whatever way feels appropriate. Does a person, place, or event come into your awareness?

Breathe into this cord, filling it with white light and expressing gratitude for its presence. Now clearly affirm in your mind: any and all energetic cords and attachments that no longer serve my highest good are cut and cleared from my body, mind, and energy. Cut and clear. Cut and clear. Cut and clear.

Breathe light into the void. Exhale any remaining debris. Inhale beautiful white light. It fills you up until it surrounds you as a protective bubble. Exhale naturally, returning your awareness to the present moment. When you are ready, open your eyes.

## *Empowering and Protecting Yourself*

Once you have done the work of releasing unnecessary and negative attachments, you should protect yourself. Sealing your aura claims your space and retrieves your power. This ensures that you are fully in charge of what comes and goes in your little universe.

## Identifying and Dealing with Psychic Vampires

Since the beginning of time, shadowy figures have loomed and crept through our minds, feeding on our essence and imprinting into our psyche. These creatures of the night embody our fears of the unknown, the seductive nature of the dark. The vampires of folklore have become nothing more than popular fantasy, or some archetypal figure of lust and total loss of control. But what if we told you vampires are real?

On a psychic level, we are constantly encountering vampires. These psychic or energy vampires, as we call them, are people who feed off of our energy and essence. Just like the vampires of folklore, psychic vampires stalk you, attach to your aura, and feed off of your essence. As sinister as it sounds, there is no blood involved, and often these "feedings" happen unbeknownst to the person being drained.

## What Is a Psychic Vampire?

Vampires represent a deeply rooted, very intense archetypal energy. They are the primal force that lives within each of us that fights for vitality and survival. These shadowy creatures feed on life force—or in most myths, blood—in order to survive. In a way, vampires are lonely creatures trying to fill the empty places of the soul.

Now take that into the real world, and we have the outlines of the psychic vampire. Psychic vampires are the very real, active personification of this mythological classic. And just like the vampires of folklore, psychic vampires feed off of your essence and your spiritual energy.

The psychic vampire is essentially an energetic parasite. They latch on to and feed from a source. They are usually a person or persons who have a weakened sense of self and a spiritual essence or aura riddled with weak spots and holes. Weakened auras and troubled mental states are invitations for the psychic vampire.

In some ways, you must take pity on those who embody the psychic vampire because it is a lonely reality whenever a person takes on the vampire archetype. They are in a world of darkness, deprivation, and despair. Energetic vampirism is born of a belief that nothing is good in the world and there isn't enough for everyone in the Universe. They are cut off from source and feed on others to fill their void.

## Detecting a Psychic Vampire

Usually a person is not aware of feeding off of others' energies. Being a psychic vampire is not usually a conscious effort. Though these people will make radical steps toward twisting, manipulating, and using people on some level, they never really know that they are grasping at a person's life force.

We would never say these people are evil. Most psychic vampires are just wounded individuals looking for a way to feel alive. Something within them has been harmed, and in an effort to find some control, they manipulate others.

Typically, there is a vampire/victim relationship. In most codependent or abusive connections, there is a vampire/victim element. The vampire is the person who is dominating and controlling. They break down the victim, feeding off of their mental and emotional energy. And on some level, the victim believes they need the vampire, though in actuality it is the vampire who needs them. As you can see, this is a two-way street. The victim has provided the space for the vampire to feed.

Psychic vampires generally come in one of two categories.

### THE MANIPULATOR

The first type of vampire is the aggressive one who manipulates and seduces you. Sometimes these types are suave and charming, and lure you in like a snake. They take you over and make you feel intoxicated. You desire their presence and, on some level, their manipulation. In terms of abusive relationships, this is usually the type of psychic vampire we see.

Often, these types of vampires are self-centered and narcissistic, and love being the center of attention. They literally suck people in and then feed off of their essence. You will find these types in powerful jobs, as they seduce their way into circles of people, infiltrating from the ground up.

They tend to be authoritative and in some ways invisible to the untrained eye. You may find yourself feeling really enchanted by these types, and though you cannot put your finger on it . . . something feels wrong about them. They check out on paper, but they just don't make you feel good!

### THE MARTYR

The other type of psychic vampire is a martyr. You will find these people always complaining "woe is me." The world has done them wrong, no one understands them, no one loves them, and no one cares about their needs. When a martyred vampire enters the room, they literally suck the beauty from it.

Any conversation you engage in with them is toxic. You feel drained just by the sound of their voice. Unlike the first type of vampires, they are not charming. It is easy to spot them a mile away from the storm of complaints around them to the negative verbal diarrhea to their unique way to make everyone feel alienated.

Sadly, some people still fall victim to the martyred vampire type because they are so persistent in their delusions that it is easy to be dominated by their view. Sometimes people even give in to these types because it is easier to "go with the flow" than to fight with them! Usually this happens if they are a family member, especially a parent or child.

## Signs of Psychic Vampirism

- Fatigue and tiredness
- Strange dreams and insomnia
- Feelings of abuse from a friend or partner
- Physical decline in health
- Mental/emotional pain and struggle
- Paranoia
- Confusion
- Sudden mood swings

- Memory loss
- Phantom feelings (cold hands, touches on the shoulder and base of spine, pain for no reason)
- Feeling fearful and afraid for no reason
- Feelings of being watched
- Accidents and clumsiness

These are just a few symptoms of being entangled with a psychic vampire. Now, be discerning when looking at this list. We are in no way advocating that everything is the result of being "bitten" by a psychic vampire. And this is not meant to create a fearful mentality. We are simply discussing the nature of the energetic exchange that happens between people.

If you have felt any of these things, ask yourself:

*Is there anyone in my life who just feels off to me?*

*Am I surrounded by people or a person who makes me feel drained?*

*Am I giving away my power to someone or something?*

*How am I honoring myself right now?*

You cannot hear this enough: you want to do what feeds your spirit and stop what drains it. When you do depleting things that dishonor your highest good, you create fertile ground for others to creep in and manipulate you.

## How to Stay Immune

A lack of personal understanding and connection to self makes you vulnerable to these energy suckers. Just like with negative energetic cords, you are allowing a path of energy exchange to exist that does not feed your spirit. But in this instance, the cord is not a two-way connection, it is a one-way street. The vampire feeds, and the victim is depleted.

When you are feeling particularly lost, down, insecure, abandoned, and just not very good, you are creating weak spots in your aura. Over time, these can become a hole or a void in which the energy suckers will take up residence. In rare cases, this could lead to you becoming a psychic vampire yourself.

Do you remember from the myth that the vampire cannot enter the home unless invited? Well, your spirit, your aura, your energy field is your home, and they cannot enter that sacred place unless you have allowed it on some level!

This makes you really want to stop doing things that no longer feed your spirit, right? When you forget your spirit, you are basically putting on a big sign that says, "I'm ripe! Come bite me!"

Start by claiming your space. Think positive thoughts, do things that affirm that you are present in your body and your spirit. Say affirmations of personal purification and compassion.

*I am loved, healthy, happy, and whole.*

*I am empowered in all areas of my life.*

*I am fulfilling my highest good, in every moment, of every day, in every way that I can.*

*I allow only good forces to enter my life.*

*Each moment, I am in full expression of my infinity and my divine spark.*

*Only good comes into my life, and that good increases in infinite ways.*

*I listen to my spirit, I feed my spirit, and I express my spirit in everything I do.*

*My life is filled with light. Infinite miracles are happening in infinite ways.*

These affirmations will reclaim your power. Anything that declares your right to your space and your divinity will banish negative influences. You will begin to mend the weak spots in your energy. When you radiate your innate light, you banish shadows. Creatures of shadow, like vampires, cannot exist in your beautiful light . . . if only you let it shine!

## Learn to Say No!

Saying no to things that disempower you will actually close the channels of communication between you and any energy suckers. Often these relationships form out of ambiguity. A boss, a friend, or a partner asks for something from you that doesn't really feed your spirit. Before you know it, you are in too deep to turn back. You are in a full-blown relationship where you are giving away power freely!

But the present moment is always the place of power. You can always say *no* right now! Keep saying no. Say no mentally. Say no aloud. And when you are in a situation that you cannot avoid, continue to put out *no* vibes until eventually the influence is eradicated.

## Parting Notes

- **Please, do not be fearful of psychic vampires.** Yes, they are very real and in our world where people can hide behind the internet and big titles. It is easy to be manipulated, but you are always in power, always beautiful, and sometimes it is the simple act of remembering your beauty that will set you free.
- **Always go back to what empowers you and feeds your spirit.** Make sure you are trusting your vibes and honoring your feelings. Avoid doing things that make you feel depleted or drained—especially when you are already feeling vulnerable.
- **Avoid drinking, smoking, and overeating**. Avoid casual sexual encounters and social interactions when you are feeling compromised. Anything that takes you out of your mind and takes you out of your spirit leaves you open.
- **Make it your daily effort to build yourself up.** Create sacred space to grow and thrive. Before you know it, your whole life will begin to glow and radiate a feeling of Universal connection!

## Spiritual Cleansing Simplicity

Many techniques exist for spiritual cleansing. Just use a tool that feels comfortable to you. And be consistent with your spiritual cleansing (whatever technique you decide to employ).

Spiritual cleansing and protection are not just an act, but a way of life. One ceremony will not make things better, but it will help. Developing a habit will fortify your energy and refine your energetic story!

## A SIMPLE SPIRITUAL CLEANSING BATH

Water has been used in spiritual cleansing for thousands of years. Baptism is in fact an ancient practice of charging water with Divine force, and bathing in it clears away the negative debris and charges you with holy light.

Water has a unique ability to hold a specific pattern of intention. Through prayer and affirmation, we charge water for spiritual work. Bathing in a tub of water filled with good intentions raises your own vibration to that of the water. It's a simple, yet powerful practice.

Run a warm bath that feels relaxing to the touch. Add in a handful of sea salt. Sea salt is a sacred mineral because it draws out and dissolves low vibrations. As with any crystalline structure, you must affirm your intention with the salt. Epsom salts can be used in place of sea salt if that is what you have available.

As the salt dissolves, envision the water glowing with golden-white light. This is the light of the Divine, however you picture it. This visualization blesses the water and charges it with spiritual intention.

Slip into the tub. Allow yourself to soak there for ten to fifteen minutes. No soap or shampoo is needed. You are not washing your body; you are cleansing your aura. You can scrub your body down with a handful of salt as an added measure.

Be sure to wet the crown and the base of your head. These are major areas for energy to slip into our aura.

Repeat a prayer or affirmation. Something from the heart is perfect.

Affirm: *Sacred water washes away all negative vibrations to reveal my luminous self.*

## A SACRED SAGE CEREMONY

Clearing and blessing through smoke is another time-honored technique, called fumigation or smudging. Burning botanicals creates smoke that will draw out negative vibes, smothering and absorbing them. Combining botanicals will clear away negative energy and infuse an aura with another intention.

Sage is sacred among the Native Americans and probably one of the best-known tools for cleansing. Smudging a home or your person with sage strips away negativity. To keep your aura flowing, add another botanical, like cedar, lavender, rose, or sweetgrass.

1. Begin by lighting a sage bundle. Once it is ignited, allow the tip to glow red. Blow the flame out, letting the leaves smolder. You can hold a fireproof bowl or shell beneath the smudge to catch any embers.
2. Waft the sage around your body, allowing the smoke to fully encompass you. I make counterclockwise circles around myself with the smudge. Sometimes I will even walk in a counterclockwise circle with the smudge in hand. Another method is to drape all of yourself except your head with a sheet and allow the smoke to collect underneath. Be careful not to burn anything!
3. Smudge your space as well. Wherever dust collects, so does negative/unintentional energy. Move through the rooms you live in, allowing the smoke to collect in corners, dark spaces, under furniture, and wherever you seem to amass clutter. You can even focus on a specific object.
4. Pray or speak affirmations while performing this ceremony. Envision the smoke absorbing and neutralizing negativity in your aura.
5. Affirm: *As this smoke gathers, all negative energy is neutralized.*

## A CLEARING CEREMONY FOR OVERCOMING ANXIETY AND EMPOWERING YOURSELF

When you are feeling really bound up and emotionally drained, clear away these energies with a special ceremony. Using the questioning technique (pages 48–49) will help you pinpoint what the source of your pain might be. Take note of where your thoughts are going or what seems to instigate them. For this ceremony, having this information will be your point of power.

You might find yourself tangled in a web of bad habits, responsibilities, past relationships, or feelings of being stuck in your life. Try to find a word, phrase, name, or sentence that clearly conveys whatever it is. There is power in naming something. We are not trying to mend things—we are cutting them away!

If you find yourself feeling completely depleted, lousy, and traumatized from a relationship, work to release it. This could be romantic or platonic, past or present. Again, you might find yourself grappling with a bad habit or a fear-based thought. Clearly name it! Gather together:

*A fresh lemon*

*A permanent marker (red or black)*

*A glass bowl filled with spring water*

*Half a cup of sea salt*

*A clean knife*

*A small white candle*

When you have your ingredients and your issue written out on a piece of paper, find a safe place where you can work. You will end up in the bathtub, so you might choose to begin there!

Begin by focusing on your breathing. Let yourself relax, unwind, and become present. Use the technique of noticing your surroundings: see, hear, smell, and feel what is in your present space. Let your breathing take you deeper, feeling your muscles relax, especially the face, eyes, mouth, neck, shoulders, and upper back. We hold so much tension there that eventually becomes toxic.

You can run through the questions listed to identify psychic vampires (*Is there anyone in my life who just feels off to me? Am I surrounded by people or a person who makes me feel drained? Am I giving away my power to someone or something? How am I honoring myself right now?*) to catapult your intention of clearing away these issues. If you want to go through this process and then reframe your statement, that is perfectly acceptable. Remember: you can do this again and again. When you have a clear statement, name, or way of describing your issue, write it on the lemon with your permanent marker.

Write in big, bold letters across the surface of the lemon! You can speak it aloud as you write it to give it more presence. Feel yourself imprinting those words across the skin of the lemon. Lemon is used in this ceremony because it has long been considered a cleansing agent in the physical and energetic sense. Connected to the moon, it helps eliminate our deepest emotions that keep us from living our highest good.

Hold the lemon in your hand and begin rubbing it over your body, as you would a bar of soap. Begin with the head, working downward in sweeping motions from head to feet. You can make as many passes as you feel guided.

As you do this, repeat this affirmation:

*I untie the bonds.*

*I release the hold.*

*I sever the connection.*

*I clear the pain.*

*I give this resistance away.*

Repeat this affirmative statement at least three times as you rub your body in downward sweeps. You are essentially sweeping your energy bodies where negative, gunked-up energies tangle your thoughts and feelings and attach you to limiting experiences.

Now, hold the lemon between your palms at heart center. Repeat the affirmation three more times. Gently squeeze the lemon, rolling it back and forth to soften the core. Let the clear aroma of the lemon fill and lift your senses.

Set the lemon aside, and begin mixing the spring water and sea salt together. Feel, sense, and imagine the bowl filling with golden light. Let the mixture pulse and radiate. This is vital, rejuvenating universal energy.

Carefully take your knife and cut the lemon in half. Repeat the affirmation above again as you do so. Let the juice drip into the water. Squeeze the two halves with your hands, draining as much juice into the bowl as you can. Let the scent invigorate you. Drop the lemon halves into the bowl.

Take your candle and wash it with the lemon-salt water. Allow the candle to dry. You can shake it or gently towel dry it to speed up the process. Hold it between both palms at your heart center.

Repeat this affirmation:

*This is the light of new beginning.*

*I am free and clear of limitations.*

*I unbind my constraints.*

*I move forward with grace.*

Light the candle.

As the candle burns, run a warm bath, soothing to the touch. Mix in the bowl of lemon-salt water as the faucet runs. Use your hand to disperse the contents so the salt dissolves and the lemon infuses all the water.

As you do, repeat:

*I am free . . . I am free . . . I AM FREE . . .*

Slip into the tub, and soak for a while. Let your tension fade, your mind release, and the energetic bonds unknot. The mixture will draw out energetic toxins and dissolve what is left of the pain. Be here as long as you need. Do not worry about washing yourself with soap or body products. Let the lemon scent, salt, and water work on you. Safely dip your head into the water. Take special care not to get lemon or salt in your eyes!

As you soak, feel yourself being free. Repeat your affirmation again or speak straight from the heart. Your spirit knows what's needed. Fill up with benevolent, glowing energy. Your spiritual light will grow and expand. You are calling back your power and potential with affirmative gestures!

Allow the candle to burn down completely. Take the remains of the lemon outside and dispose of them in the trash or near a tree's base. Let the ghosts of your past issues, heartache, and pain remain there, in the past . . . in the trash. You're free!

This ceremony feels cathartic, liberating, and completely empowering. When we talk about working with intentions, we need actions to set them into motion. This clearing ceremony helps you acknowledge, name, and consciously give away whatever is holding you back. You can move forward in this way only if you are brave and ready for change. You are magic, and the Universe helps those who wish to help themselves.

Afterward, you will feel *lighter, brighter,* and more *alive.* You may need time alone for introspection. You have done some deeply healing work. Be gentle, compassionate, and aware of those needs. Sleep, rest, sing, walk. Remember, you can return here as often as you like. If you are dealing with an especially difficult situation, repeating this for three consecutive days is advisable—or longer. Trust your inner wisdom. Do other supportive work alongside this to bring about balance, composure, and clarity. Self-care is a lifelong commitment.

Always follow up your spiritual cleansing with a protective measure.

### SPIRITUAL PROTECTION VISUALIZATION

Spiritual protection fills in spaces opened up by your cleansing. It seals in good vibes and keeps negativity away! Spiritual protection allows you to continue claiming space and reinforces your intentions.

Though there are many ways of sealing and protecting yourself, using white light is a tried-and-true method. Visualizing white light calls on Divine energy to surround you in a bubble of protection. This is especially helpful in public places or high-intensity situations.

1. Close your eyes. Focus on your breathing. Find your rhythm. Begin to inhale to the count of four and exhale to the count of four.
2. Imagine a waterfall of golden-white light pouring around you. See yourself wrapped in, encased by, and protected by this Divine light.
3. Affirm: *I am surrounded by the white light of protection, love, and healing.*

Use the white light whenever you need. Anytime and anywhere, the white light of protection will surround you!

### VISUALIZE ULTRAVIOLET LIGHT

Ultraviolet light is a spectrum of light that is outside of our visible range. This light radiates in a unique way that interacts with everything on a molecular level. It basically radiates low vibrations, and on a physical level, this spectrum of light will kill bacteria and other illnesses.

Visualizing this light surrounding your body will help to eliminate negative influences and protect you from intruders. Energetically, ultraviolet light will raise you to the vibration of your highest good.

Ultraviolet light is related to the upper chakras, especially the crown. You will actually perceive this spectrum of light around spiritual figures and what are called ascended masters. When you align with this energy, you are aligning with your own divinity.

Like the white light of protection we often hear about, ultraviolet light can be visualized as a protective barrier. Throughout the day, especially when you are feeling particularly vulnerable, imagine this light around you.

## VISUALIZE A CLOAK OF BLACK VELVET

Black is a powerful color for diffusing psychic interference. Essentially, black is the absence of color, a void that absorbs and silences energetic turbulence. This color promotes psychic protection, transformation, and gestation.

Begin to calm yourself through rhythmic breathing. Find your personal flow, inhaling to the count of four, then exhaling to the count of four. Place your hand on your belly, feeling it rise and fall with your breath. Spend a moment going deeper into your body, your mind, and your spirit.

Once you've found your center of gravity, fill your mind with static. See the static like on an old TV, crackling through your head, and allow your mind to hum. Let it grow and expand through you, around you until you are absorbed in a salt-and-pepper static snowstorm.

Now that you are in the center of this static cloud, notice the black specks beginning to outnumber the white. Growing, thriving, and multiplying, the static begins to turn a deep, velvety black, leaving you cradled in a soothing, soft cloud of darkness.

You are now shielded from harm in a warm black velvet cloak of protection. Every negative intention or stray thought that floats into your personal space will be absorbed into the blackness of your velvety cloak, recycled back into the Universe to be used somewhere else.

Wearing a black sweater, a velvet jacket, or a nice black wool scarf will amplify this visualization, something soft, soothing, and warm that you can wrap yourself in. Remember, you can recall your velvet cloak visualization whenever you need.

## BLACK TOURMALINE, THE PROTECTOR

Black tourmaline is one of the most revered protective amulets. This deep, inky black stone is often rough and variegated. Wearing black tourmaline has an effect similar to the velvet cloak of protection. This stone will neutralize psychic interference and help clarify the atmosphere around you, shielding and protecting you from negative intentions and even malevolent forces.

Deeply shamanic, black tourmaline will energetically root you in the earth and help you go inward for meditation and introspection. In this state of reflection, you will find clarity and understanding of your thoughts, emotions, and energetic story. Going inward allows you to also discover your spiritual purpose and claim your space on all levels.

Wear black tourmaline in pieces of jewelry or tucked into a small leather bag around your neck or waist or carry it in your pocket. Hold it during times of need. Even tucking it under your pillow while you sleep will allow its magic to work! Listen to your intuition and the stone's spirit.

### CALL UPON YOUR SPIRIT GUIDES

Don't forget to call on your Spirit Circle for help! Your spirit guides, angels, and all other celestial helpers are always willing to step in on your behalf. They can give you protection and offer insight into whatever you are working on.

### DO THIS DAILY

Create a daily practice of drawing awareness to your energetic state. Paying attention to this idea of energetic cords is only one way of claiming your sacred space. See what works for you. Always be patient and gentle with yourself. Self-love heals and raises our vibration.

## *Play Your Part in the Universe*

Here are just a few tips for building up your spiritual immunity and also doing your part in the Universe. There are so many ways to spread good vibes and help inspire love and creativity, so start with these but also find what works for you. Most importantly, listen to Spirit's messages for you. You have a unique way of being in the world, and often that is the most powerful tool for abolishing negative energy!

## Playing with Intentions

You've found yourself playing in the present moment. You are taking notice of how you are feeling and allowing yourself to go deeper into the state to see why. That is the best question you can ask yourself in daily life: *Why?* Why am I feeling this way? Why am I stuck on this? Why does this make me feel good? Why is this important?

*Sometimes simply asking why is all you need to do.* No lengthy answer is needed. The question itself is a call back to the present. Just remember if you are not feeling good vibes, then your spirit is saying to go in a different direction. Put one foot in front of the other and begin shifting your intention. Small intentions gesture change.

In this present moment, as you are sensing your whole being, you discover how you feel. But how do you *want* to feel?

Focusing on how you want to feel in your life is the foundation to creating everything else. Your deepest intention begins with a feeling. That feeling is the seed you plant in the fertile grounds of the Universe to grow into a whole experience. *So how do you want to feel?*

Ask that question throughout the day and see how far away from that feeling you currently are. When you want to feel love, but frustration is all you can muster, ground yourself in the moment. Feel that frustration. Really breathe it in, let it move through you, and then allow it to cycle out. We have to release our feelings by experiencing them, not ignoring them.

Then you can move on to the next best feeling! And on and on it goes, like climbing a ladder.

## Self-Compassion Kindles Self-Expression

Practice speaking to yourself kindly. Use affirmations, prayers, and poetry to feed your spirit. Surround yourself with things that make you feel beautiful and alive. Your home and work space are sacred and should glow with an atmosphere of good feeling.

Try the following affirmations daily:

*I live a magical life of authentic self-expression.*

*I am loving myself more and more each day.*

*I honor my inner wisdom and the beauty of my soul.*

*Empowering opportunities are coming to me in infinite ways.*

You can also write your own to reflect your unique path of healing and self-expression!

## Exalting the Jewels of Your Soul

Now you have a glimmering jewel of wisdom, a beautiful intention you can act upon. Begin to build a world around this Divine intention. Give it life, color, texture, and a name. This can happen in whatever way you see fit. You could create a vision board of this desire so you can see it with your physical eyes. Or you can write about it. Whatever way you can explore this desire will feed your spirit.

Small steps toward your desires are all that is required. You do not have to make radical changes. Let the path unfold before you as you grow more interested and trusting of your feelings. When the voice of fear pops up, soothe it by saying: "Right now, I am playing with intention!"

## Making a Pact with Your Dreams

Sometimes, our dreams and desires don't match the life we have lived so far. We look in the mirror and say, "I don't look like a (rock star, artist, preacher, dancer, etc.)." In your mind, you don't live up to the image you are wanting to become, so you shy away from it. Though you may not have been born a prodigy, singing since you came from the womb, or painting or writing, that doesn't mean that you can't start working toward any of these today.

Your dreams are your personal treasure, and only you can determine whether you will fulfill them.

Make a pact with yourself, in the night, by the water, in the moonlight.

Make a special pact with yourself on a star, that you will give your dreams and talents a little spark of life. Begin to believe in the longing that you have. The Universe gave you a special spark, and that spark is meant to ignite a fire within that illuminates your world.

People speak of destiny as some contract written in stone. That is his destiny, that is your destiny, that is my destiny. Your destiny is determined, not by your luck, but by your longing . . . the things you yearn for, the things that make you light up, the things you dream about. Those are the things that hold the key to your destiny.

Destiny isn't a set of things to achieve; destiny is a state of awareness you expand to.

To make your dreams come true, you must start with a small gesture. You must wave to the Universe, saying, "Hey there! I am ready to open the door for this dream." This isn't to say you have to turn your life on its side and change everything, but you can create a focal point for this new energy. Allow the door to open in your mind and heart, and then it will reflect into the physical world.

Here is an exercise:

Collect a small pile of images and words that highlight a deep burning and desired dream. Find images that hold the energetic vibration of what you are creating. Now find a good card stock and cut out a circle. It can be any size, but make it big enough that you can fit your images on it and still clearly see them.

This will be your mandala, which is basically a meditation wheel for inspired focus. On this circle, you will collage your images in a way that moves you. On the back, write the date, an affirmation that highlights your desire, and your signature.

As you empower this mandala with your intention and repeat your affirmation, you are imbuing it with powerful energy. Your signature is a declaration to the Universe that you are making a pact with your dreams.

At least once a day, take a few minutes to be with your mandala. Feel through the images, the words, and colors. Let them sink in deep and digest into your spirit. Feed your soul with this inspired intention.

Allow these feelings to well up inside and pour into the mandala. Your mandala serves as a reminder, a type of energy vortex that burns into your life the opportunities you need to achieve these dreams.

The more open you are to the Universal spirit, the more open it can be to you.

## The Power of Possibility

Once you set your intention by rooting it into a feeling, open it to possibility. No matter what you feel or the circumstances you find yourself in, the one thing you can always trust is possibility. *There is always the possibility for something else to come.* That is the nature of the Universe!

Hold that feeling of possibility deep inside of you. You don't need to worry about what shape that possibility will take. That only diminishes its power. The Universe knows how to take a seed and grow a tree and then a forest without any help. Paths will unfold before you, bringing you situations and experiences that you could never imagine. So why waste the energy trying to force things?

It is not enough to be outraged. When something bothers you deeply, be curious enough to find out why. Something within *you* needs expression. The outside world made you aware of this need.

As you light the flame of your inner vision, others all over the world will do the same. And we have no reason to find the light, because we become the light—the light of change that illuminates the dark and the guiding star that glows in the eye of the storm.

PART TWO

# THE TAROT

## *A Mirror on the Self*

*Now that we've confronted the shadow and looked at ways to see all parts of ourselves, it is time to learn about the deeper information the Tarot can provide. Tarot holds a mirror up to our selves, and when we engage with the insights we find there, we can take a significant step in healing ourselves and healing the world.*

# 4

# Introducing the Archetypes

It's time to introduce you to your new ally on this path of discovery and healing: the Tarot archetypes. Each archetype is embodied and portrayed by one of the twenty-two Major Arcana cards. As you explore their imagery and descriptions, you will discover how each card operates both in light (expressed) and shadow (avoided) aspects.

As you read through each description, you may find yourself recognizing aspects of your own life and personality. If you identify more with the shadow side of your archetype, do not judge yourself. Keep an open mind and be willing to acknowledge this part of you. The cards are just a mirror to reveal your challenges and gifts and all the different ways to grow your power and potential.

Remember: at some point in everyone's life, they will move between the light and shadow parts of their archetype. Let this insight wash over you and open your awareness to something deeper, bigger, and more enriching than what you knew before.

Although you will have one main archetype based on your Birth Card calculation, you may find that you identify with others too. The Tarot is universal, as are these archetypes, and ultimately, all the qualities the cards share are within the spectrum of our potential as human and spiritual beings.

You'll notice how all of the archetypes show up within yourself and your own experience. As you learn more through this chapter, explore what that looks like in real time. How have you embodied the creative potential of the Magician? When are you forceful like the Emperor? How can you be vulnerable like the Star?

You will find a level of comfort or familiarity with certain archetypes. You'll have the distinct feeling of seeing yourself in the personality of that card. But there is also power in exploring what opposes, triggers, or pains you in the description of other cards. Be with this experience and always ask yourself: How can I grow from this?

As you'll see, no one will ever be the Fool because birth dates will never add up to zero. However, you may at some time consider choosing this archetype to work with, especially if you are beginning a new chapter in your life. So instead of zero, we will be using the number 22 for the Fool.

## *Tarot Birth Cards as Archetypes*

The Tarot offers unlimited ways to explore ourselves and the world around us to gain understanding, clarity, and a sense of direction. The Major Arcana shares insight and wisdom regarding the major themes we experience on a global and completely personal level. These cards can be used as guiding constellations to understand the unique challenges and blessings that life will present in order to grow our spirits, our perspective, and our sense of purpose.

Just as you were born under the influence of a particular sign of the zodiac, you also have a particular Tarot card that embodies your life theme. Calculating this Birth Card offers a unique opportunity to understand your experience, to see the wisdom hidden in your challenges, and to reveal the different paths to awaken your sense of purpose.

Keep in mind that nothing is set in stone: your Birth Card serves only to open you up to new ideas and prompt you into action. Approach this practice with the curiosity to inquire about your own unique purpose and expression in this world and how this relates to the Tarot. Let yourself be moved to grow and show up bigger for yourself and the world.

### Calculating Your Birth Card

Begin by adding together all of the digits that make up your birthday, including the year. The sum total will correspond to one of the twenty-two Major Arcana cards. In this instance, we treat the Fool (0) as card 22.

> For example: If your birthday is February 3, 1990, you would calculate your Birth Card by adding 2 + 3 + 1 + 9 + 9 + 0, which would total 24.

If the sum of your birthday is higher than 22, distill it down by adding the digits again.

For example: 24 would be 2 + 4 = 6, making the Birth Card for this date the Lovers (6).

The Lovers reveals that this person will be sensitive to the choices that are being made in each experience, and they may have trouble knowing what would be a healthy choice to support their well-being, which could lead to indecision and not wanting to commit.

A supportive affirmation would be: "I easily make choices that support my well-being."

Understanding your Birth Card in this way reveals how you can grow and be more on purpose, as well as the challenges you could encounter and means to overcome them.

Some people will have two archetypes based on the way numbers may be reduced—or not. An example of this would be if your birth date boiled down to 13. Number 13 is Death. You could choose to work with that card, or you could further reduce the number 13 down to 4, which would be the Emperor.

Theresa's birth date adds up to 11, which is Justice. She shares how that has manifested in her life:

> Back when I was younger, I was concerned with injustice and actually toyed with the idea of being a lawyer. I was involved with some social justice work for a time, but then my path took a different turn—and I stepped into the role of a Tarot reader, which I have been now doing for almost thirty years. When you reduce 11, it becomes 2, the number of the High Priestess. I vibrate strongly with this number, but there are times when I still go into Justice mode!

## Choosing to Work with Other Archetypes

A core aspect of *Tarot for Troubled Times* is knowing you can grow your light. Seeing every experience as an opportunity to ask questions that expand your awareness is fundamental. Growth and personal evolution are the key to your overall well-being, so adopt the mantra: *I am curious.* With each archetype, ask questions that take you deeper, stretch you wider, and inspire you to action. Remember this not only with these exercises, but also in life as a whole.

As you become acquainted with your Birth Card, possibilities will show up for you. You'll have a clearer understanding of yourself and the energies guiding your life. This can be a power step forward into living purposefully and thriving in your life.

You might find your Birth Card deeply resonates with you. You already connect with the profound energetic platform it provides, and you want to grow deeper into that expression. On the other hand, your Birth Card might challenge you with creative prompts for growing your light and cultivating more conscious actions in your life you've never dreamed about.

Both can hold true depending on your present perspective and the situation you find yourself in. Life isn't a vacuum, and different circumstances evoke different expressions of your unique qualities and capabilities.

However, there is another path to empowerment—and the building blocks of true magic in your life. You always have a choice because no one thing can completely define you. Your Birth Card is a mirror for you to explore the reflection of your infinite self. But what if another card calls to you?

As you read through the qualities for each card, another constellation might speak to you. If that happens, choose to go deeper into that experience and find the wisdom it holds. Trust your intuition when something grabs your attention. Choosing to explore deeper possibilities lets you become a big player in your own life!

## Different Ways to Reveal the Potential of the Archetypes for You

As you explore the Major Arcana archetypes, notice which cards beyond your Birth Card attract or repel you. There is power in both experiences. When something attracts you, it wants to become part of the web of your experience. When something repels you, it serves to teach you where you can pivot, open, and change.

With an intention in mind, look for cards that embody what you'd like to heal, change, create, or integrate into your life. Intention is the power piece for all change in life. As you become clear about your intention, you see avenues toward actualizing it manifesting. Intention must be met with action to create change. What is your intention? What card displays qualities and actions that help you get there? How can you embody those qualities?

When you find a card that embodies the qualities that feel appropriate and aligned with your intention, pull it from your deck and keep it on your mirror, altar, or nightstand as a reminder that you are capable of doing the same. See this card as yourself and meditate on or visualize yourself as the archetype doing exactly what you intend to do. This is a great way to use your affirmations!

Pinpoint where you need healing. Healing on all levels begins by making a commitment to shift your experience and take steps toward mending wounds and releasing traumas. Wounds can be physical challenges, emotional baggage, past traumas, or resistant beliefs. Notice which card embodies or holds facets of wounds you would like to mend. Example: When challenged by male authority, see what qualities of the Emperor you can learn from, make peace with, or incorporate into your life. Often, the antidote to pain is making peace with the poison.

If you find a particular card that depicts an aspect of your trauma, use the other cards in the deck to visually express the story around that wound. From there, you can change the story by adding new cards that resonate with how you'd like the story to be told. This will edit the energetic web around that trauma and allow you to heal and integrate the shadow and the light.

The archetypes are messengers and teachers. If you desire to learn more about how to be, feel, act, or display a new quality within yourself, find an archetype to teach you. You might see Strength as a teacher of overcoming adversity. How does she do that? What can she show you? Or you might seek the High Priestess's wise counsel to develop your psychic gifts. Pay attention to how they embody those skills and what they do to use them. Make a list of actions you can take as instructed by this teacher.

## The Archetypes

### 1 MAGICIAN

Unlike the Fool, the Magician knows what he's doing. He's got mad skills and the willpower to manifest exactly what he wants. His tools are laid out in front of him, and he uses them to create the reality he desires. This is self-command, innovation, and focused will. The Magician stands in his power, knowing that he, and only he, is responsible for what shows up in his life. By aligning spirit and matter, he manifests his destiny.

The shadow side of the Magician is trickery, abuse of power, a lack of focus, and manipulation. Instead of relying on the tools, resources, and talent available, he resorts to chicanery.

## 2 HIGH PRIESTESS

The High Priestess knows what's up. She's intuitive and empathic, and always trusts her instincts. She's a keeper of secrets and a shape-shifter. As an archetype, she is feminine wisdom embodied. When she's ready, she freely shares her knowledge. But most of the time? It's hidden away behind her pomegranate curtain, to only be shared with a select few deemed worthy.

The shadow side of the High Priestess is passivity, sneakiness, making assumptions, or an inability to trust intuition. Instead of confidence in her instincts, she seeks advice from others. This can lead her off the spiritual path. Dark secrets that need to come out in the open can be another shadowy High Priestess vibe.

## 3 EMPRESS

The second female archetype in the Major Arcana is the lovely Empress. She's the nurturer and protector of the young and vulnerable. Like Mother Earth, she is creative and fertile—and she takes care of her own. A true matriarch, the Empress cares deeply for all, but she's not all benevolence and motherliness—she is also sensuous and enjoys pleasure. Living life to the hilt? That's her. She's large and in charge—and not afraid to say so.

The shadow side of the Empress is smothering and neediness. Think of the overbearing helicopter mom or the martyr who caters to others without thinking of her own needs. Get the picture?

## 4 EMPEROR

Like the Empress, the Emperor protects and provides well. But his energy is Yang, paternal, and disciplined. His motto: he who makes the gold makes the rules. He's the boss! This archetype is the authority figure who rules the kingdom. Under his leadership, everything is safe and stable. You're in good hands! He's a fearless leader, matured from time spent in the battlefield, and ready to assume his seat of power.

The shadow side of the Emperor is the control freak who wants to dominate. Instead of providing safety, he takes away the rights of others and lacks empathy. Force is his weapon and rules are bent to serve his needs. This is the energy of oppression, misogyny, and the patriarchy.

## 5 HIEROPHANT

The Hierophant is the spiritual teacher, the person who takes the rules of the gods and brings them down to earth. He is society's moral compass. Tradition and structure are important to him. Like the Emperor and Empress, he's in a position of authority. In this case, he's in charge of ethics and spiritual wisdom.

The shadow side of the Hierophant is blind faith, conformity, intolerance, and a rigid, dogmatic belief system. The false prophet using spirituality to control others or the obedient sheep drinking the Kool-Aid are both shadowy elements of the Hierophant.

## 6 LOVERS

The Lovers archetype is dualistic in nature. On one hand, this card symbolizes attraction and union. The other hand is concerned with choice. What choices are going to serve your highest good? How will you integrate both options? Life is a series of choices, and the Lovers say to choose between temptation or the gods. This archetype is also love incarnate—as in love for your fellow man. It's a reminder that love is the law. Without love, life feels empty.

The shadow side of the Lovers is indecision, indulgence, infidelity, giving in to temptation or lust without thought of repercussions. The person who uses others for personal gratification is an example of the shadow of the Lovers.

## 7 CHARIOT

The archetype for the Chariot is the hero returning from battle, victorious and in control. He's not afraid to take charge or to dive into a fight. Likewise, he lives his life like a true warrior: fighting for what's right . . . and what's his. If this is your archetype, you're in the driver's seat, and you, and only you, can decide how far you'll go. You are a champion!

The shadow side of the Chariot is aggression, misplaced willpower, lack of direction, or issues around control. And it's not just about trying to be in control, but in some cases, losing control. If you've ever given your power to someone else, you know the shadow side of the Chariot.

## 8 STRENGTH

Although the Chariot has power, so does the Strength card. But here, there is no need for force. Instead, this card symbolizes the power within, the feminine use of potency. Instead of aggression, the heroine employs gentle, but firm, energy. This archetype is the female magician who needs no tools, but only her hands to make magic happen. She is the female leader who uses love to win the war.

The shadow side of Strength is a lack of courage or a ferocious, untamed ego. The energy here can be overbearing but weak at the same time. The father who harshly disciplines his children but can't stand up to his ogre of a boss is an example. A victim mind-set is another shadow archetype of the Strength card.

## 9 HERMIT

When we need to pull back from the world, we are living the Hermit archetype. This is the card for spiritual wisdom and introspection. The wizened one, the recluse, who carries both mystical and earthly knowledge gained from experience and looking within is pure Hermit energy. He is both seeker and teacher, looking inside and out for the truth. Solitude? No biggie. It's where the best information arises.

The shadow side of the Hermit is someone who cannot be alone, doesn't trust their inner guidance, or is dependent on a guru. Also those who never learn from their past mistakes are shadowy Hermits, as well as those who close off the world and refuse to engage. The loner who can't operate in society would be a shadow archetype of the Hermit.

## 10 WHEEL OF FORTUNE

Lady Luck and opportunity are associated with the Wheel of Fortune. The archetype here is fate and change, the ability to go with the flow. No matter whether life is up or down, the Wheel continues to go around. At its best, it recognizes opportunities and seizes the day. It is the toss of the dice, the gamble that produces a big win. The Wheel of Fortune archetype is also the catalyst that begins a movement.

The shadow side of the Wheel of Fortune is resistance, woe-is-me, and blaming troubles on "bad luck" rather than taking responsibility for not grasping opportunity when it was presented.

Refusing to budge or move with the times—that's it in a nutshell.

## 11 JUSTICE

As an archetype, Justice is concerned with fairness and equality for all. This card symbolizes knowing right from wrong—and the laws of humankind. Like the Lovers, this card also indicates choices; in this case, it's about doing the right thing, no matter what. Those who fight for the rights of others are operating on Justice energy. These are the people who set the laws that protect society.

The shadow side of Justice is an inability to take personal responsibility or to accept the consequences of actions in the past. Instead of standing up, they cry "no fair" and blame others for their problems. Or they work to oppress. Unethical, shady, or illegal actions are also the shadow side of Justice. The crooked lawyer or corrupt judge is an example of Justice's shadow.

## 12 HANGED MAN

The worthy sacrifice, that person who gives up everything for the good of everyone else—this is the Hanged Man archetype. This card symbolizes patience and faith—that inner knowing and trust that what is being given up will come back in higher ways. Being able to see things from a different point of view is also Hanged Man energy.

The shadow side of the Hanged Man is the martyr. This is the person who makes unnecessary sacrifices, who cannot trust in the universe, or who cannot let go. Instead of faith, doubt rules the roost. Have you ever been so filled with skepticism that you cannot see the miracles around you? If you have, you know the shadow side of the Hanged Man.

## 13 DEATH

The Death card is the agent of change. This archetype is here to transform, which means clearing away the old and outworn to make way for the new. Endings and new beginnings are part of this card. Get the ball rolling or get out of the way for those who want to bring change. The revolution is coming and this card brings it.

The shadow side of Death is the fear of change, inertia, or being so hung up on the old way that you cannot see the new. So you hang on for dear life and hope that nothing evolves. Or you rage at those who are bringing about the necessary societal changes because you're worried that you'll be left behind—or left footing the bill.

## 14 TEMPERANCE

The Temperance card is the alchemist. Here, lead is turned into gold, water into wine, and so forth. Moderation and balance lead to the center. Patience is the virtue of Temperance. The ability to skillfully mix things up in a peaceful way is the talent. Diplomacy and a willingness to hear all sides are Temperance in action.

The shadow side of Temperance is feeling out of balance, overindulgence, and a lack of patience. When you overdo anything, you're working with the shadow energy of this card. Also, intolerance—the inability to hear another point of view—is another side to this Tarot shadow.

## 15 DEVIL

The Devil is the ultimate shadow card! The energy here is dark and oppressive. But the power comes when we face those dark spots and realize that the chains are loose—and we can remove them. In short: personal responsibility and a willingness to own up to our mistakes are how we can work with this card.

The shadow side of this ultra-shadowy fellow is materialism, oppression, addiction, victim mentality, abuse, hatred, and fear. Forcing others to bend to your will as you maintain all the control and hoard all the wealth is a manifestation of the Devil's shadow.

## 16 TOWER

The Tower is the catalyst, the bulldozer that tears down the old to raze a space for the new. Like the Death card, this one favors change, but here the energy becomes one of revolution. Chaos reigns with this card, but it can be a portal for growth. Things come to a head and the walls come tumbling down. From there, a new order can rise.

The shadow side of the Tower is resistance, clinging to the old ways, anger, or repressing feelings. It's the bloody revolution that arises when people refuse to give up their power for the good of all. Marie Antoinette with her "Let them eat cake" is an example of the Tower's shadow. It's corrupt power that meets a bloody end.

## 17 STAR

The maiden in the Star symbolizes hope and healing, which makes this archetype the healer or bringer of light. After the darkness of the Devil and the Tower, the Star reminds us that there is good in the world and a reason for living. Inspiration and transformation are the positive aspects of this card. People who give us reason to believe in good things are the positive side of the Star.

The shadow side of the Star is feeling hopeless or being out of touch with reality. A Pollyanna attitude of unwillingness to explore the truth of the situation is nothing more than avoidance. It's the head in the sand that sees nothing, does nothing. Instead of inspiring, the shadow of the Star loses her light and gets stuck in the dark. Debbie Downer would be an example of the Star's shadow.

## 18 MOON

As an archetype, the Moon symbolizes change and instinct. Those times when the world goes dark and we cannot see, but have only the light within ourselves to guide us are full of Moon energy. There will always be times when the path becomes treacherous, but we must not give up or give in to fear. Instead, we must find the light in the darkness, and that starts with turning inward. Looking within will reveal the truth. This card is as mysterious as can be and a reminder that life isn't always what it seems to be.

The shadow side of the Moon is doubt, anxiety, the inability to see, and holding back out of fear. Remaining in your comfort zone because the world looks too scary means the work needed doesn't get done.

## 19 SUN

This glorious card is a reminder that life is good and worth living. The archetype here is the joyful child who spreads happiness wherever they go. Playful and creative, they inspire others to feel good. Like the Star, the Sun is a symbol of hope and a reminder that things can be bright again. This card carries the energy of the inner child, as well as rebirth. Passion and success are also attributes of the Sun.

The shadow side of the Sun is a refusal to see joy, negativity, the inability to find happiness, and the loss of childlike wonder. When you neglect your inner child, you do not allow this energy to shine fully.

## 20 JUDGMENT

The moment arrives, and the revelation is here at last. The Judgment card points to an awakening, a time when the truth is obvious. The higher calling is evident, and now that you've received the call, you must follow. Transformation is at hand: shed the old and rise up to a new beginning. Forgive the past, welcome the new. Transcend!

The shadow side of Judgment is a critical attitude, poor decisions, a disconnection from spirit, and a refusal to answer the call. The person who is quick to judge others, but unable to see their own transgressions, is operating in Judgment's shadow.

## 21 WORLD

The World signals the end of the journey or spiritual graduation. This is being at one with the world and universal love. Here, all are welcome, integrated, and safe. The chapter closes, and another dance begins. Perfection and peace are here at last. It's unity. Everything has come home.

The shadow side of the World is limbo. Rather than closing down the old, everything is up in the air. An inability to finish what's started or to open up to new possibilities are both shadow sides to this card, as is the habit of letting the world's problems get to you. Sometimes we need to be in the world, but not of it.

## 22 FOOL

The Fool leaps into experiences without a care in the world. He's innocent, yet his knapsack and wand suggest that he has experience. This card represents our treasured innocence and the side of us that moves through life with total openness, ready for wherever the adventure takes us. As an archetype, the Fool symbolizes curiosity, uninhibited actions, starting fresh, and exploring uncharted territory.

The shadow side of the Fool is ignorance, reckless behavior, fear, distrust, lacking attention, holding back, or stepping blindly into danger. As the saying goes: fools rush in where angels fear to tread.

## *Working with Your Archetype*

The archetypes we've looked at have suggested affirmations, keywords for the positive as well as the shadow side, plus suggested actions you may want to take that might help you make an impact on the greater collective. Let's explore how to get to know your archetype and get to its personal impact. Then let's look at the Personal Year Card, which shows what energy is operating in your life from year to year. By combining your archetype from your Birth Card with your Personal Year Card, you can navigate your world in a way that makes sense for you with presence in the present. Because ultimately, that's what this is all about: awareness. The more aware you are of your nature and the energy around you, the more you can show up present, healthy, and totally authentic.

### Using the Birth Card Prescriptive Affirmations

Your Birth Card offers a guiding constellation for your life that embodies the unique expression you are meant to share with the world. Each Birth Card has an accompanying prescriptive affirmation that holds the essence of the card's message. By integrating this essence into your daily life, you ignite your inner fire and activate your internal compass to point you in the right direction. Using this prescriptive affirmation rewrites the inner dialogue that runs through your subconscious mind and turns on your innate energetic magnetism, placing you in the position of power and empowerment.

- **Notice how the affirmation resonates with you.** Each affirmation is an energetic prescription meant to align you with your purpose so you can thrive, express, and truly live in the flow. Sometimes these affirmations will feel opposed to your core beliefs. In this case, become curious. Ask yourself why you feel challenged by this new pattern of thinking and feeling. You are always in the place of power to rewrite your internal narrative. Try to pivot your perspective, lean into the experience, and allow something new. If the affirmation deeply resonates with you, ask yourself how you can take it deeper. How can you make this a guiding light in your daily life?

- **Journal on the affirmation.** Allow the affirmation to open a new way of thinking, feeling, seeing, and believing. Write out your initial thoughts about the affirmation. What comes up for you? Where have you felt this sense of purpose before in your life? How can you grow into this new flow?

- **Write the affirmation.** Write out the affirmation on a sheet of paper in clear, bold, and inviting script. Place the affirmation where you will see it daily. Consider having a copy on your vanity, in your car, at your desk. Shaheen relates his personal experience with affirmations: I love to write affirmations on my mirror in bold colors with lipstick or chalk pens so that I can read them each time I look into it. You cannot help but notice them. You may also want to create a reminder on your cell phone so that the affirmation pops up throughout your day!

- **Repeat the affirmation.** Repetition is a powerful way to align your energy with your intention; intention without action is fruitless. Begin and end your day by repeating your affirmation ten times. When you notice you are in resistance and feeling stuck in some way, repeat the affirmation to bring you back to center.

- **Write new affirmations.** Use your Birth Card Affirmation as an entry point into your unique purpose. Begin going deeper by asking questions. How can you bring this into your life? How can you shift and change? What supportive thoughts and beliefs will help you get there faster? Use the actions as a catalyst to go bigger, level up, and make change. Remember: Intention + Action = Results!

- **Be kind to yourself.** There is no rush to the finish line. Each moment of your life will be met with new experiences and new possibilities. Your path and purpose will evolve every step of the way. Take your time and hold space for yourself to be curious.

## How to Take Action

As you acknowledge your shadow and begin working on the healing process through the prescriptive affirmations, you may find yourself feeling empowered—and ready to inspire others! After all, it's great to step into your power, but even more divine to take this energy out into the world. If you already have experience as a change-maker, this work will help you to be more effective.

But what if you don't? What if you want to make a difference, but aren't sure how you can best serve? Stepping into the role of leader or activist may seem daunting, but it doesn't need to be. Each Birth Card has an action that you may want to consider. These suggested actions will give you an idea of how to best express the energy of your archetype out in the world.

For example, if you're the Magician, you may be extremely effective at stepping into a leadership role in your community, whereas a High Priestess may be happier working behind the scenes of a political campaign. The Empress might enjoy focusing on the needs of the younger generation, while the Emperor may want to start a nonprofit or run for office.

Keep in mind that these are just suggestions. We are diverse, and each one of us will have different abilities, schedules, health, or financial situations. If none of these prompts resonate, find something that makes sense for your Birth Card and your life. *Be you* in the way that feels right.

# 1 MAGICIAN

**Affirmation:** "I create my reality."

**Positive:** skill, willpower, ability to manifest your desires, focus, standing in your power

**Shadow:** trickery, abusing power, lack of focus

**Actions:** Take on a leadership role in your community; stand up to bullies; make some noise!

# 2 HIGH PRIESTESS

**Affirmation:** "I follow my intuition."

**Positive:** intuitive, sensitive, feminine

**Shadow:** passive, makes assumptions, unable to trust intuition

**Actions:** Work behind the scenes, perhaps in a political campaign; share your wisdom; donate resources.

# 3 EMPRESS

**Affirmation:** "I have enough."

**Positive:** nurturing, caring, creative

**Shadow:** smothering, neediness, ignores own needs

**Actions:** Nurture your community; get involved in Big Brothers/Big Sisters programs; be an advocate or mentor for the younger generation.

# 4 EMPEROR

**Affirmation:** "I am in control of my life."

**Positive:** disciplined, stable, control, authority

**Shadow:** control freak, domination, lacking empathy, force

**Actions:** Run for office; start a nonprofit; lead a good cause.

# 5 HIEROPHANT

**Affirmation:** "I am supported by infinite wisdom."

**Positive:** spiritual, mentor, teacher

**Shadow:** uptight, rigid, dogmatic, blind faith, conformity, intolerance

**Actions:** Give to charities; take on a mentorship role; teach others.

# 6 LOVERS

**Affirmation:** "I easily make choices that support my well-being."

**Positive:** romantic, communicative, makes healthy choices

**Shadow:** indecisive, unable to resist temptation, indulgent, infidelity

**Actions:** Bring people together; listen to the other side; mediate conflicts in your community.

# 7 CHARIOT

**Affirmation:** "I have a clear sense of direction."

**Positive:** willpower, direction, responsibility

**Shadow:** lack self-control or trying to control matters, no direction, misplaced aggression

**Actions:** Protest; start a campaign; lead where you can.

# 8 STRENGTH

**Affirmation:** "I use empathy over force to navigate conflict."

**Positive:** strong, patient, able to handle conflicts and trials with grace

**Shadow:** overbearing, lack courage, weak, ego

**Actions:** Confront bigots; stand up to bullies; take care of those who feel marginalized; be a voice for the oppressed; let people lean on you.

# 9 HERMIT

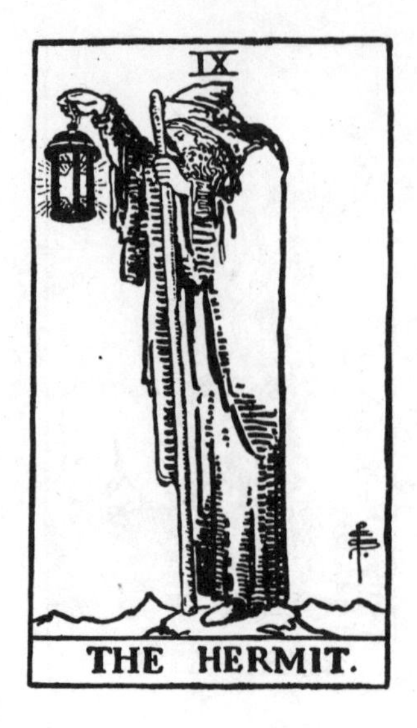


**Affirmation:** "I honor my need for introspection."

**Positive:** wise, in touch with inner wisdom, introspection

**Shadow:** cannot be alone, out of touch with inner guidance, dependent on a guru, fearful of others, not learning from mistakes

**Actions:** Learn as much as you can about current events—seek knowledge; teach what you know.

# 10 WHEEL OF FORTUNE

**Affirmation:** "I move with the flow of the Universe."

**Positive:** recognizes opportunities, change-maker, goes with the flow

**Shadow:** resists change, woe-is-me mind-set, blames fate or bad luck

**Actions:** Start a movement; join a movement; be an advocate for big changes in your community.

# 11 JUSTICE

**Affirmation:** "I lead from a place of integrity and wisdom."

**Positive:** fair, just, makes sound decisions, integrity, balanced

**Shadow:** inability to take personal responsibility, cannot accept consequences of actions, thinks life is unfair, lack of integrity

**Actions:** Demand justice; petition your government; contact representatives; educate people about injustices; get involved with causes that fight for civil and human rights.

# 12 HANGED MAN

**Affirmation:** "I am flexible with my perspective."

**Positive:** able to let go, sees things in different ways, goes with the flow

**Shadow:** hang-ups, unnecessary sacrifices, inability to let go and trust the universe

**Actions:** Gain a new perspective by spending time with someone who has a completely different point of view; try to see the other side; give something up for others; donate time or money.

# 13 DEATH

**Affirmation:** "I honor the process of change."

**Positive:** creates and welcomes change, can let go, open to possibility

**Shadow:** fears change, inertia, stuck in past, can't let go

**Actions:** Be an agent of change; confront the old ways; initiate new movements; advocate for change.

# 14 TEMPERANCE

**Affirmation:** "I am balanced."

**Positive:** balanced, patient, moderate

**Shadow:** feeling out of balance, not moderate, overindulgence and addiction

**Actions:** Join a peace movement; march; mediate conflicts.

# 15 DEVIL

**Affirmation:** "I learn from my shadow."

**Positive:** recognizing and taking personal responsibility for problems, faces the shadow

**Shadow:** addiction, chained to fear, power issues, victim mentality, blames everyone else, feeling stuck

**Actions:** Confront your own prejudices and work to change from within; petition to get corporate money out of politics; confront and question powers that be.

# 16 TOWER

**Affirmation:** "I have a solid foundation."

**Positive:** revolution, liberation, able to tear down to rebuild

**Shadow:** fear of change, resistance, freaking out, repressing anger

**Actions:** Start a revolution; protest; march; confront violence and injustice; demand politicians be held accountable; stand up to corporations.

# 17 STAR

**Affirmation:** "I am grace."

**Positive:** hope, inspiration, healing, transformation, positivity

**Shadow:** Pollyanna attitude, imbalance, feeling hopeless, out of touch with reality

**Actions:** Spread a message of hope; promote peace; be a light for others.

# 18 MOON

**Affirmation:** "I honor my feelings on all levels."

**Positive:** strong instincts, navigate tricky situations, in touch with feelings, sees the shadow

**Shadow:** doubt, confusion, unable to see through the fog, resisting the shadow

**Actions:** Work behind the scenes on a campaign or good cause; confront false information; shed light on what's true.

# 19 SUN

**Affirmation:** "I am filled with abundance in all forms."

**Positive:** joyful, abundant, successful, play, creativity, inner child

**Shadow:** neglects inner child, lack of joy, refuses to see joy, negativity, lack of creativity

**Actions:** Focus on children's needs; spread optimism; share your wealth by contributing to good causes.

# 20 JUDGMENT

**Affirmation:** "I am awakened to my higher purpose."

**Positive:** makes good decisions, follows higher calling, good critical faculties, rebirth and transformation

**Shadow:** overly critical of others as well as self, faulty judgment, disconnected from spirit, refusal to answer higher calling

**Actions:** Be a messenger where you can; encourage others through example; send a message to your representatives; speak up!

# 21 WORLD

**Affirmation:** "I am centered."

**Positive:** success, completion, finishing a cycle, being at one with the world

**Shadow:** inability to finish a chapter, hanging on to the old, letting the world's problems get under your skin, a myopic vision

**Actions:** See the world; welcome other cultures into your life; get involved in global causes or the environment; take care of Mother Earth and the climate.

# 22 (0) FOOL

**Affirmation:** "I trust the Universe."

**Positive:** curiosity, uninhibited actions, leap of faith, exploring uncharted territory

**Shadow:** reckless behavior, stepping into danger, lacking attention, distrust

**Actions:** Learn more about diversity; get out of your comfort zone; get educated.

## *Working with Your Year Card*

Every year, the energy shifts. The wheel is always in motion. Life presents us with new gifts and challenges, which helps us to continue to grow. Nothing ever remains static—including us.

We must learn to work with change, using our own strengths and wisdom to move forward in the way that is aligned with our higher guidance and makes the most sense for us. Each one of us will react to what's happening in our lives in our own unique way.

When you understand what energy is operating for the year, you can deal with the issues and max out the gifts.

Each year, a different Major Arcana card influences the energy around you. When you calculate this card, you will be aware of what your major themes are—and how to cope.

### How to Figure Out Your Personal Year Card

Add the digits of your birth month and day with the digits of the current year. If the number is greater than 22, add the digits again to reduce it to a number from 1 to 22.

> For example: If you were born on July 23, here is how you would find out the number for 2019: 7 + 2 + 3 + 2 + 0 + 1 + 9 = 24. Because 24 is greater than 22, this would need to be further reduced: 2 + 4 = 6.
>
> Six is connected to the Lovers, which means your Personal Year will be governed by this card.

Some numbers will leave you with multiple options, which gives you the opportunity to decide which energy makes the most sense for your year. For example, if you get 13, you can choose to consider Death or reduce it to 4, which would be the Emperor.

Because it's impossible to have a "zero year," we will treat the Fool as number 22.

For each card, you'll find positive and negative manifestations of your Personal Year Card along with a possible affirmation. These are merely suggestions. As the year continues to unfold, you will begin to see how the energy is showing up in your personal life.

You may wonder: does my year begin on my birthday or at the turn of the year? You can choose whatever makes the most sense for you. Some people have found the turn of the year sets the tone for them, while others feel the birthday is more accurate. Experiment and see what feels right.

# 1 MAGICIAN

**Affirmation:** "I am a powerful being."

**Positive:** This is your year to step into your power. Real magic can happen now. Begin the year by setting your intention. What do you want to have, do, or be? Put a clear intention out into the world, and then remain focused all year until you see the manifestation of your goal. This is also a fantastic year for developing your skills. Take a class, find a mentor, be diligent with your practice. The more you work on your talents, the more proficient you'll be. This is also a year to speak your truth. If you have something to say, do not hold back. Stand firmly in your power and lead with confidence.

**Shadow:** using shortcuts to get what you want, abusing your power or refusing to accept it, opting for trickery instead of work, lack of focus, fear of standing up or standing out

# 2 HIGH PRIESTESS

**Affirmation:** "My intuition perfectly guides me."

**Positive:** You have the gift of intuition all year long. This will give you the edge in making decisions. Before making a move, consult with your own inner wisdom. It will not steer you wrong. If you are uncomfortable trusting your gut, this year may give you the validation you need to finally start listening. All of the knowledge you need is contained within you. Do not seek out others for advice. Instead, look within. This year may also find people confiding in you. You are able to keep secrets and provide wise counsel, so this should come as no surprise. Your ability to see the truth of the matter and offer kind understanding gives you the gift of wise compassion.

**Shadow:** hiding, fear, keeping secrets out of shame, passiveness, an unwillingness to get involved when you should, a refusal to listen to your better instincts

# 3 EMPRESS

**Affirmation:** "I take care of myself and those who need me."

**Positive:** In the Empress year, you may find yourself playing a nurturing role for others. This may be your family, friends, or perhaps people at work. Take care of others, but make sure that you are also taking good care of yourself. The Empress is a sensual card, making this year a feast for the senses. Indulge in the things that give you pleasure. Surround yourself with beauty and creature comforts. You'll be rich with creative ideas all year long. Act on those ideas, and you may grow something beautiful. Lastly, much can get done if you are willing to put in the work. If you take the initiative, you can be quite productive, and this can lead to a good harvest later in the year.

**Shadow:** putting everyone else's needs before your own, playing the martyr, overindulging to the point where you put on weight or deplete your resources, laziness, the helicopter mom who can't cut the apron strings

# 4 EMPEROR

**Affirmation:** "I am willing to take charge of my life."

**Positive:** This is your year to take charge. Up your game. Take the lead. Be the authority even if only the authority of your own life. Discipline will be required this year. You have the ability to build a solid foundation. If you are willing to do the work, you can go far now. Recognition is possible, so do not be afraid to step up and take matters into your own hands. Others may look up to you this year. Do what you can to provide security or inspiration. The energy of this card is paternal, which means rules and protection are vibrating strongly. This is the right time to set the terms and make sure everyone follows along. You're the boss!

**Shadow:** irresponsibility, bossiness, dominating others, insensitivity, controlling behavior, rebelling against the rules

# 5 HIEROPHANT

**Affirmation:** "I teach what I know."

**Positive:** The Hierophant is the spiritual authority, which means this year you may want to reflect on your spiritual traditions. What sustains you? Are you connected to a particular faith or are you ready to create your own dogma? This is a strong year for developing your philosophy. Seek a mentor. Look for a spiritual teacher that you trust and ask the big "meaning of life" questions. You may also find yourself in a position where people want to learn from you. Share your wisdom and trust that you have the answers too. This year is also ideal for any sort of learning. Whether you're going back to school or simply discovering a new skill on your own, focus on education, and you'll reap many benefits.

**Shadow:** intolerance, bigotry, turning over your power to a guru, bucking the status quo, a rigid attitude, bowing to "the man"

# 6 LOVERS

**Affirmation:** "My choices are based on love."

**Positive:** The Lovers year is focused on partnerships—and not just romantic ones. This is your year to examine all of the relationships in your life. Are they healthy? Do you need to communicate better? Are you giving as well as you get—and getting as well as you give? Reflect on how you are showing up in relationships and how others are showing up for you. Seek to find compromise where you can. In some cases, you may need to set boundaries. There may also be new rules to negotiate. The more willing you are to do the work, the better your relationships will be. This year can also bring love. If you've been alone, the Lovers year promises the potential for companionship. Of course, this starts by loving yourself. When you love yourself completely, you open the door for the right people to come into your life. The Lovers also indicates major choices. The decisions you make this year may have far-reaching consequences. Consider your options carefully and think about the impact each choice may have. Always choose mindfully . . . and with love.

**Shadow:** communication breakdown, boundary issues, selfishness, feeling alone, self-loathing, allowing others to walk all over you, making poor choices

# 7 CHARIOT

**Affirmation:** "I am in control of my destiny."

**Positive:** The Chariot signals willpower and progress. The reins are firmly in your hands this year. Where do you want to go? What is your biggest goal? Set your sights on the future and go, go, go. You can make great progress on anything you choose. Even if you encounter a few difficulties, you will find the detours and reach your destination. There may be times when you need to travel. Feel free to indulge in your wanderlust as much as you can. If you are thinking of moving or changing your path, you can do so without too many issues. Remember: you're in the driver's seat. If you want a different future, you can make that choice this year. This is also a good year to practice standing in your personal power. If others try to manipulate you, be strong. Put on your armor and take control of matters. You are unstoppable!

**Shadow:** giving up control, controlling others, a lack of direction, wanting to turn over the reins to someone else instead of taking charge, an unwillingness to handle the present challenges

# 8 STRENGTH

**Affirmation:** "I am able to handle whatever life throws at me."

**Positive:** This year will bring tests, but if you trust in your own inner power, you'll tackle these with grace. It may seem to take every fiber in your being to manage at times, but do know that you'll prevail. The key here is to not give up. You must persist with a gentle, but firm awareness until the problems are wrangled. The Strength card can indicate the struggle within. Are you the source of your own problems? If so, it's time to get out of your own way so that you can succeed. Look within and see how you're tripping your own self up. Then, do what you can to regain control of matters. This year can bring great healing and triumph, but that begins when you recognize how you set yourself up for failure or success and then taking control. There are times when others will need you this year. You do have the capacity to help others. In some way, helping them could be a way of helping yourself. Be courageous and put your heart into the things you want. You may be surprised to see that you can get great clarity and success if you channel these qualities.

**Shadow:** forcing the issue, dominating others, giving up, letting your animal nature take over, creating unnecessary drama, being a bully

# 9 HERMIT

**Affirmation:** "I am wise."

**Positive:** The Hermit year is perfect for introspection. Instead of looking outward, this year requires an inward focus. You may have to withdraw from certain activities in order to do this. Or it may be that situations arise that find you having more time to yourself. That time alone will be good for you, so soak it up. Learn to love your own company this year. Above all, look at your life. Are you happy with the path you're on? If not, seek answers through contemplation or working with a trusted teacher. This year requires inner reflection instead of outer action. Don't push. Rest up when you can. Next year will bring some amazing changes. This is the year to get ready for those.

**Shadow:** fear of being alone, isolation, ignoring your own inner wisdom, not learning from the past, repeating your past mistakes due to a refusal to get the clue

# 10 WHEEL OF FORTUNE

**Affirmation:** "Every change I experience moves me in the right direction."

**Positive:** This year will be pivotal, so get ready! Everything is poised to change. The ball has already been set in motion, and things are rolling as they should. Momentum is at hand, and you must trust that the Universe is moving you in the right direction. Certain elements of this year may feel fated. A greater force may be at work. Ups and downs are possible, but if you are open to the changes around you, you'll navigate even the trickiest situations. Lady Luck may present you with a few interesting opportunities. Should you take them? Sure! It may turn out to be fortunate indeed. This year will be a roller coaster at times. At other times, it will be a game of chance. Toss the dice—you're winning!

**Shadow:** feeling a lack of control, losing momentum, an unfortunate turn of events, making stupid decisions, taking foolish risks, resistance to change, blaming others for your bad luck

# 11 JUSTICE

**Affirmation:** "I do the right thing."

**Positive:** When Justice is your card for the year, it's a sign that the laws of karma are balancing out. The consequences for decisions made in the past will now come due. You reap what you sow. Know that no matter what is happening in your life, it's fair and just. Take responsibility for your decisions of the past and, if necessary, correct your course. It's also important that you examine all of your choices with great care this year, for decisions made now may change your destiny for good or ill. This year requires tremendous amounts of patience, responsibility, and mindfulness. If you bring these qualities forward, you may see things turning in your favor. The Justice card can sometimes indicate legal issues. If you are dealing with any sort of legal matter, be careful. Scrutinize all the details, and if you're not sure, get advice from an attorney.

**Shadow:** irresponsibility, blaming others for your problems, unfairness, illegal activities, poor decision-making, lack of integrity

# 12 HANGED MAN

**Affirmation:** "I let go and put my trust in the Universe."

**Positive:** The Hanged Man year is never easy, but if you lean into it, you will gain a whole new perspective. This year requires release. You must let go and put your trust in the Universe. This may not be easy to do, but once you surrender and release the need for control, things will begin to fall in place. You may be letting go of certain situations, habits, people, or beliefs. Know that this will be for your highest good. Sacrifices will also be required. You may need to put others first. Also get ready to be the bigger person in some situations. Others may act a certain way, but you must remain in your integrity at all times. The Hanged Man is also a card of limbo, meaning many things may seem to be on hold this year. There may be nothing you can do about that except wait it out. By year's end, you'll gain a whole new outlook on life—and have a greater connection to your spiritual life. All those sacrifices and letting go of stuff? Totally worth it.

**Shadow:** martyr issues, persecution complex, feeling stuck, holding on for dear life, lack of faith

# 13 DEATH

**Affirmation:** "I am ready to let go of the old so the new can arrive."

**Positive:** This year will bring major change. What's old and outworn will be fading out of the picture, and it's important that you go along with this process. Transformation is possible, but you must be willing to let go of all of the remnants of the old you. You may be called to release things that feel important, such as a long-term relationship or a habit that you've clung to for many years. You must trust that whatever is moving into the past is for the best. (It is.) Burn a few bridges this year. Tear down the old structures. Shed your skin. Say goodbye to toxic relationships and aspects of your life that no longer fit. Declutter every area of your life. Purge. By the time this year comes to an end, you'll be shorn, clean, clear, and completely transformed. And up ahead will be new growth and possibilities.

**Shadow:** fear of change, resisting the inevitable, holding on to things or people that you've outgrown, stubbornness

# 14 TEMPERANCE

**Affirmation:** "I am creating something new."

**Positive:** After last year's Death card, Temperance indicates a year where you can put the pieces back together in a whole new way. Think of this as alchemy: what do you want your life to look like? What pieces of the old life might you integrate into the new one you're creating? The energy is creative and meditative—an opportunity to thoughtfully arrange your life in a way that is aligned with your highest good. Often, this can only be achieved after an upheaval. This year, look at what elements you want to keep from the old life and what new ones you wish to introduce. Experiment. You can find the perfect blend if you approach this mindfully. This year may bring some important decisions. Weigh your options with care. Does it fit the life you are creating? Let that help you determine the best choice for you. This year may also find you traveling or spending time near water. These can be spiritual practices for you or simply balm for the soul.

**Shadow:** an unbalanced life, indecision, feeling wishy-washy, a half-assed approach to things, losing faith, going to extremes

# 15 DEVIL

**Affirmation:** "I face my shadow with courage."

**Positive:** This year can be fabulous for indulging in your desires or exploring your dark side. Hedonistic tendencies could find you taking things to the extreme: overeating, spending beyond your means, or having multiple sexual partners. Keep a leash on your temptations; lust and desire can lead you to the negative side of this card, which is addiction. If you feel you are heading that way, know that you alone will be responsible for liberating yourself, and you possess the resources necessary to get out. The Devil year is the best one for shadow work. Go deep into your shadow issues—anger, fear, addiction, obsession, and control. By facing these aspects of yourself, you can make peace with them and experience breakthroughs. This card can also symbolize important, consequential choices; this year, you may be choosing between the devil you know and the devil you don't know. Pick wisely. Themes of power are another attribute of this card. How do you approach power or use it? Does it scare you? Do you wield your power with grace or control? Explore your relationship to power and see what role it plays in your life. Let your use of power be a source of light for all to see.

**Shadow:** anger, addiction, oppression, overindulgence, issues around control and power, poor decision-making

# 16 TOWER

**Affirmation:** "I am liberated."

**Positive:** You can be sure that your life will be going through a massive shift when the Tower is your yearly card. This is a time for revolution, for tearing down the old so that new structures can be built. Anything that ends this year will be for your highest good. You must trust this even if you feel uncertain or scared. It's likely that you will experience many breakthroughs and aha moments. But those breakthroughs cannot arrive unless a breakdown occurs. Be ready to tear things to the ground, to the roots. Clear away the debris. Release what blocks you. Say bye to old, stale relationships. When all is said and done, you'll have a clean slate to work with. Then you can begin creating the future you want. Epiphanies you receive this year will help you determine exactly what that needs to look like. You are free to make a fresh start.

**Shadow:** fear, anxiety, disruption, accidents, a fall from grace, violence, anarchy

# 17 STAR

**Affirmation:** "I am hopeful."

**Positive:** After the destructive Tower year, the Star brings hope back into the picture. Now you can see the bright side of things. Optimism is returning, and better yet, things are ready to heal. The breakdown is now paving the way for many breakthroughs and opportunities. This year may bring about many of your deepest wishes. Set your intentions at the beginning of the year, remain positive, and watch the magic unfold. Others may look to you for inspiration. Do not be afraid to shine. Instead, put yourself out there fully. Be visible. Set the example of what it means to be positive. If last year felt like a crisis, this one will be deeply healing and inspiring. Life is good. Believe in magic and know that what you want is totally achievable this year.

**Shadow:** losing hope, pessimism, giving up, lost in fantasy, refusing to face reality, lack of opportunity, wishes squandered

# 18 MOON

**Affirmation:** "I am fearless."

**Positive:** The Moon is dark and mysterious, which means things may not be clear this year. Instead of a well-lit path, things are dim. You'll need to trust your instincts going forward. Even if you cannot see what's ahead, your gut will help you to avoid danger. Listen to the wisdom of your inner voice, and you'll navigate your challenges with precision. Fear and sensitivity are both present now. Other people's problems could get under your skin. Learning how to be present without getting sucked in will be one of the many challenges that this year presents. Boundaries will be tested, and you'll need to be on guard at all times. Dreams and intuition will be especially strong now. Pay attention to the messages you are receiving, for there is much wisdom within. This year can also bring illusions. Things and people may not be what they seem. Look beneath the surface. Wait until you get more facts. Take your time. Soon enough, you'll see what's up. Then you'll be able to move quickly toward your destination, much wiser for the journey.

**Shadow:** fear, illusion, anxiety, seeing only what you want to see, boundary issues, not trusting your gut when you should

# 19 SUN

**Affirmation:** "My future is bright."

**Positive:** This year, success is yours for the taking, for the Sun indicates everything is possible. Abundance, opportunity, and pure potential are present, which means this year could find you living your dream life. This is your time to shine brightly, go for what you want, and remain optimistic. Look at the sunny side of things as often as possible. Let joy be your everyday waking state. Follow your bliss and have faith in your dreams. It's possible that this year could bring financial gain, fame, or the birth of a child. It's also likely that new projects and opportunities may land in your lap. What you touch can turn to gold. Luck is on your side and life is good. You are the golden child this year, so do expect most things will go the way you want. Keep a sense of play and wonder around you. All is moving in the right direction.

**Shadow:** immaturity, acting like a brat, pessimism, coldness, burnout, not taking advantage of opportunities

# 20 JUDGMENT

**Affirmation:** "I am reborn into a new state of perfection."

**Positive:** Judgment signals the end of a chapter. Something is coming to a close this year. This is the end of one way so that a new one can begin. It's possible that something may be finalized, giving you an opportunity to reflect on what was before moving on to what may be. Closure is possible if you are willing to shed the old. There is no need to hang on to the past—this must be released if you want to rise up to your full potential. In a way, you're going through a transformation. This is a time when you are seeing things in a whole new light. Revelations and epiphanies will bring clarity. A whole new way of looking at the world will be yours by the time the year ends. You are at an important crossroads: examine the old life and begin to explore the new directions that are beckoning. You may find your true calling this year. Or you may simply find the courage you need to let go of old habits, relationships, and stories so you can begin anew. Do trust your judgment this year. If you see a new way or a problem, know that your higher guidance will help you to make the best possible decision.

**Shadow:** refusing the call, holding on to the past, resistance, judgmental attitude, unwillingness to evolve

# 21 WORLD

**Affirmation:** "I am complete."

**Positive:** The World signals a year of success. Something important is being completed this year. It may be that you finish an important project or reach a goal that you've been working at for a long time. This could be something to do with your work or your personal life. The World symbolizes a graduation. This could be graduating from school or a spiritual graduation of sorts. Know that you are going to ace any test that comes your way, because you've been building your skills through the experiences of the last few years. In a way, you're getting the satisfactory closure that you have been craving. As you finish your goals, you need to ask yourself, what's next? World travel is a possibility in the World year. If you've wanted to broaden your horizons by seeing the world, this is your time to do so. Whatever you do this year, do it big. The world is watching. Lastly, do not be afraid to be in the spotlight. After all, you've earned that right to be there.

**Shadow:** failure, not learning the big lessons, lack of closure, limbo, unfinished business, being without direction

# 22 (0) FOOL

**Affirmation:** "I am ready for change."

**Positive:** This year brings a chance for a fresh start. If you have ever wanted to begin anew, this is your time. The Fool year is ideal for leaving behind the baggage of the past and lightening your load. If you're thinking about moving or making a major change, this card says: go for it! Take a risk and see what happens. A curious and open mind-set is needed at this time. No matter how much experience you have gathered over the years, this year calls for beginner's mind. If you can, travel as much as possible. See the world. Broaden your horizons by going where you've never gone before.

**Shadow:** taking foolish risks, ignoring responsibilities, acting the fool, refusing to make necessary changes, clinging to the past

## *Journaling Exercises*

Find the Birth Card archetypes of world leaders.

How does each archetype fit them?

Can you see both the positive aspects and the shadow side of this person?

Next, find their Personal Year.

How are they showing up in the world?

If you could give them advice, what would that be? Journal your thoughts.

## *Recommended Reading*

*Who Are You in the Tarot?* by Mary K. Greer. This is an in-depth look at Tarot's Birth Cards.

# 5

# It's Elemental

Although the archetypes of the Major Arcana are the main focus of the inner and societal work we're doing, the elements must not be overlooked. They, too, hold an important role. By exploring them, we can find practical ways to support the work we're doing.

## *What Are the Four Elements?*

The four elements are different realms that hold their own unique energy and potential. Think of them like different phases of a cycle. One element can roll into the next. You might vacillate between different elemental energies or stay in one for long periods because it nourishes you, feels natural to you, or has become your comfort zone.

The elements work symbolically, energetically, or/and environmentally as the personification of something or someone or as steps of development.

Understanding which element is dominant in your energetic story will help you see where you are in process and how you've invested your energy. This reveals your attention and intention and illuminates your actions.

## *The Four Suits of Tarot and the Creative Process*

- **Wands represent Fire:** Ruling action, creativity, energy, potential, birth, ambition, expansion, expression, and charisma.

- **Cups represent Water:** Ruling emotions, feelings, love, relationships, subtle worlds, memories, intuition, and spirit.
- **Swords represent Air:** Ruling the mind, mental states, thoughts, conflicts, communication, projection, and force.
- **Pentacles represent Earth:** Ruling the material world, money, success, career, business, sustenance, and physical manifestation.

## Creative Process

The Minor Arcana expresses the creative process, showing the progression of development, formation, articulation, and manifestation. We are always in one or more phases of this process. As you practice working with the Tarot to heal and empower yourself, look for actionable steps you can take to become a participant in the creative process. Not only does each card hold a special energetic vibration, but each element can also offer a magical action to take.

- **Potential** (Wands): Fire is the primal, creative force that lives in the core, unexpressed potential of a seed bubbling with life. It holds the power of new life, beginnings, and the point of origin. It is abstract clay waiting to be handled. Utilize the element of fire for creating and transmuting facets of your life by performing magical work with fire, such as burning written petitions, lighting candles, or heating things up.
- **Analysis** (Swords): Air offers direction and forward motion. Rational thought organizes possible application. Experimentation involves observing, testing, reworking. Utilize the element of air to gain momentum, direct change, and hone in on possibilities by performing magical work with air, such as lighting incense to shift the vibration around you, using aromatherapy or scents to hone in on your intention, or releasing things to the winds to be carried away.
- **Inspiration** (Cups): Water is a surging, fluid, and creative force. It is inspiration flooding into awareness. It is the tingling of the senses,

enticing intimacy with feelings and emotions. It is new life kicking in the womb. It is playing with disparate connections. Utilize the element of water to deepen your experience, nourish your intentions, or wash away debris by incorporating water into magical work, such as bathing with herbs and oils, drinking teas and liquids, or creating elixirs that align with your desire.

- **Manifestation** (Pentacles): Earth energy solidifies what was only potential. Something has formed from nothing. It is the fruits of your labor held in your hands. Abstract energy trickles into inspiration, then action, and now life. Utilize the element of earth to solidify your intention and manifest whatever you desire by working magic with the element of earth, such as hand making charms and talismans, growing plants from seeds that have been imbued with your desire, or incorporating crystal medicine into your self-care practice.

## THE GARDEN OF OUR LIVES

Shaheen's grandmother had a strong connection to the earth and the elements:

"When I contemplate the four elements, I am reminded of my childhood working with and watching my grandmother create her garden. The chill of winter would blanket the land, killing and freezing any hint of life left on the surface. My grandmother would work diligently, dreaming and planning from a warm window overlooking her flower beds, dreaming of the blooms, fruits, and vegetables she would plant in the spring.

When spring came, she would clear, tidy, and till the land to reveal the rich soil where she'd plant her desires. Each seed she'd collected in jars from the previous year would be lovingly placed in the earth and covered with care. Warm sun and fresh water would feed the seedlings, and she would tend to them daily until everything burst and bloomed into life, with every color of the rainbow floating atop a sea of green.

Throughout the summer and into the fall, she would harvest her riches. She would can the vegetables, freeze the sweet fruit, and dry the flowers, all the while gathering seeds for the following year.

As the year came to an end, she would lay her garden to rest with care and attention so she could do it all over again. Her commitment to gardening was her art, her way of life, and a meditation on the process of birth, death, and rebirth. Clearly the four elements were at work in my grandmother's garden. Her Birth Card is the Lovers.

If you imagine your life as a garden, you can begin to see the elemental forces that are always present and the different phases or stages of your own unfolding process.

If you can reclaim the sacred moments in everyday life and notice the ebb and flow of energy you are investing, you can regain full recognition of your immense power. Your garden of desire is planted with seeds of intention moment to moment. Whether you know it or not, you cradle the seeds of your very creation with every thought, idea, feeling, and belief you give yourself.

The four elements teach us how to be present and connected to our power. You are always investing energy with your intention or attention and your actions. View each element through the lens of your archetype and the reason for your inquiry.

You can always begin by asking yourself:

*Where am I being nourished?*

*Where am I being depleted?*

## FIRE. WANDS. SPIRIT. INSPIRATION. POTENTIAL.

Fire eradicates, dispels, and ignites intention.

The suit of Wands embodies fire. Wands funnel and direct power through action and intention. Fire is an active energy that bursts with raw, hot potential. As the raw creative force that tempers, shapes, and transforms, fire can come as a strike of lightning, a bolt of inspiration that awakens every part of the self before it sinks into your awareness.

When you explore the realm of fire through the Wands, you are sinking into the primal, animating force that moves through all of us. Fire could be called the spark of life—the latent potential burrowed in the shell of a seed, such as in the Ace of Wands. It holds the power of new life and a new way of being. Or it can be the burnout from too many coals in the fire, as in the Ten of Wands.

Light a candle and watch the flame bob, hop, and dance on the wick. Feel the warm glow fill the room and your inner space with a generative force. You can warm yourself in the firelight, gently basking in the glow. Within the flicker of a flame you can thaw the bitter cold of sorrow or incinerate the heart with deep desire.

Imagine if the candle tipped over. The flames would become deadly, burning and consuming everything in sight. There is an unruly, unpredictable nature to fire. In this way fire can eradicate or even dispel the darkness, the undergrowth, and the fodder.

You are a candle that can be ignited by the power of fire. Regardless of where our power lies or how we use the potential of fire, the truth remains that we are strong, capable, and even destructive.

When Wand cards appear, pay attention to the creative energy moving through you. You are ripe with potential and ready for action. Bask in the flow of fire to enliven your spirit. What spark of inspiration is being ignited within you? What ideas are you being called to explore intellectually and intuitively? What actions are you being pushed to take? What fodder or debris in your life could be transmuted into fertile space for new life and creation? What are you plugged in to?

To work with fire energy, light a fresh candle that you've filled with your wish, prayer, or desire. Watch it dance and glow brightly. Know that your intention will be drawn to the flame of your spirit. Maybe you need to calm the fire or clear away the old. Begin by writing out whatever weighs on you, by either making a list or composing a letter. Then burn the paper to release the pent-up energy and contemplate the stillness and potential left in the ashes.

### WATER. CUPS. EMOTION. INTUITION. INSPIRATION. GESTATION.

Water cleanses, washes, nourishes, and awakens the heart.

The suit of Cups represents the qualities of water. Water can cleanse, release, nourish, and awaken. Water feeds the seedlings of intention. Our deep traumas and emotions can pulse under the current of our lives until they find a crack to gush through and flood the surface. Freely flowing and finding the path of least resistance, water opens the caverns of the heart to feed channels of love, desire, and fantasy.

A cup can hold your changing, fluid emotions, where you can gaze upon their surface to gain entry into the deeper wisdom of your psyche, such as the Queen of

Cups lost in reverie. Other times, you are lost in your wild imagination, imbibing fears and fantasies like the shadowed figure of the Seven of Cups.

If you watch the ocean at night, you can see the immense potential of water. Tides wash in, carrying treasures, lost artifacts, and an array of enigmatic things. When the tides draw out, they carry with them whatever lies on the shore to be mixed into the vast unknown of the ocean. Cradled in the womb of the ocean are relics of the past, wonders of nature, and unimaginable dangers.

The realm of water is a pervasive ocean with no land in sight, calm on the surface with a whole world of strange and mysterious experiences awaiting underneath. Yet it can also be the last drop of water sizzling in the sun on a parched and barren land. Floating on calm tides lulls you into a trance of rejuvenating sleep to refresh the heart and soul. But the right weather can turn your blue, calm sea into thrashing waves that lick the solid foundation of life until everything is obliterated.

Relentless and unrestrained or placid and composed, our emotions have the power to nourish or destroy us. You can be moved by the tides of love or flooded by the rush of hate. With water, you should make time for stillness and reflection. Follow the current of your emotions, and you'll find where you need to be.

When Cup cards appear, they entice intimacy with your heart-space and your emotions. Find time for stillness and contemplation, where you can dip into the sacred waters of your inner world and play with disparate connections. What are you feeling right now? What does your heart long for? How is your intuition prompting you? Does anything from your past keep bubbling up to the surface? What can you rinse from your heart and life right now?

Work with water by drawing a warm and soothing bath. Add a calming essential oil to it, such as lavender or sandalwood. Slip into the tub's embrace, close your eyes, and let the tranquil buoyancy and healing scent take you deeper into your feelings. Notice whatever comes up for you. If you are overcome by your emotions, take a meditative walk to somewhere in nature and bring along a fresh water bottle. Find a place that feels inviting and sit in silence, expressing your emotions to Spirit. When you are finished, pour a libation of water on the ground, thanking Spirit for mending your heavy heart.

## AIR. SWORDS. MIND. ANALYSIS. EPIPHANY.

Air moves, shifts, and transforms our thoughts.

Air is symbolized by the suit of Swords. This element holds the power of mind and intellect. Air can shift, shape, and transform everything around it, and in this way, our mind is a tool for calculation and analysis. Wield the sword with intention to effect change, but if you use it carelessly, it becomes a tool of destruction. Mental precision is the difference between success and failure.

Swords are emblems of battle, defense, and calculation. If you take a deeper look at this implication, you can see the progressive nature of air and how it can take you further and higher, and give you momentum. Getting trapped in your thoughts and beliefs can lead to restlessness, depression, and mental fatigue, such as in the Nine of Swords. When you take ownership of your mind, you can plan and strategize with clarity, like the King of Swords.

Our passing thoughts can blow through our minds like a warm and gentle breeze in the spring. Left unchecked, our thoughts and beliefs can be a destructive tornado ripping through our lives, uprooting our sense of security and foundation. In time, wind can erode solid stone and mountain peaks, the same way our limiting beliefs can eat away at our personal well-being.

If you watch fluffy clouds floating overhead, you can enjoy the process of observing. See your thoughts in this way. Allow them to fill your mind. Observe what potential they might hold and then look for connections. Thoughts can transform like clouds, so allow your mind to be an open space for experimentation. If you can observe your thoughts, they will prompt further clarity and expansion, carrying you to the next phase of your life. However, if you let your thoughts and beliefs rule you, your mind becomes an iron maiden.

Your mental state can be tumultuous and destructive. Sometimes you blow about, lost and confused by too much thinking. Other times, you are compelled to follow the direction of an idea. Let the power of air keep you flexible so you can plan, test, and calculate your ideas with ease. Know when the winds of change are blowing to avoid too much time in your head where every thought becomes noxious and polluted.

When Sword cards appear in your life, notice where your head is and take stock of your thoughts and ideas. You are entering a phase of change though observation and analysis. Test and experiment, formulate a plan, and explore the ways to execute it. What thoughts and ideas keep appearing in your mind? How are your thoughts and beliefs moving you forward? How are they harming you? What is your plan of action?

To work with the element of air, take some time for mindful breathing. Simply sit and observe your thoughts. Let them pass through you like clouds. Notice which ones entice you to explore further. You can write them down. This is a wonderful way to solve problems and plan ahead. If you're crippled by too much thinking and battling anxiety, stop for a moment and ask . . . is this thing I am thinking really true? Then notice what you smell, what you hear, what you feel, and what you see around you. Close your eyes and ease into the moment.

## EARTH. PENTACLES. BODY. BIRTH. MANIFESTATION.

Earth grounds, centers, and solidifies intention.

Pentacles or Coins are the emblem of earth energy. Earth is the solid foundation our lives are built upon and the womb of creation, regeneration, and rebirth. We plant the seeds of our livelihood within the belly of the ground and nurture them into life. With respect, we bury our dead to be wrapped in the restful embrace of earth. If you see the earth as womb, and the womb as a doorway or passage to new or different ways of being, you discover the immense power of the suit of Pentacles. Pentacles are the fruit of our labor, the currency we exchange for goods, and the seeds of promise we hold so dear.

The energy of earth is found in the Pentacles as different stages of material life, labor, and worldly experience. Dig deeper into this symbolism, and earth becomes a metaphor for the body. Our bodies are the accumulation of our life experience, from our trauma, pain, and failures to our rites of passage, pleasure, and well-being. Barren earth is a sign of trauma brought on by abuse of resources, greed for personal satisfaction, and neglect and deprivation. Fertile earth grows green and wild from unification, mindfulness, and respect for the cycle of give and take.

Strong, enduring, and tenacious, you are like the earth. You can feel tortured, mutilated, and utterly desperate for soothing like the Five of Pentacles. You might stand in a rich garden, ripe and luscious with vibrant fruit, and luxurious like the Nine of Pentacles. Other times, you are the Four of Pentacles, overcome by fear, lack mentality, and frugality, holding tightly to what you have at hand. Regardless of your experience, the promise of change is always present. When you hold the talisman of Pentacles, you're reminded of the power inside to rest, regenerate, and reclaim your life, your health, your body, and your experience.

Pentacles ask you to be present, patient, committed, and alive with your own nature. Be like the earth that shakes and rattles to free herself of the oppression and restraints placed upon her. Frozen, barren, and forgotten, you still hum inside with a spark of life. Sprout like the relentless weeds in the cracks on a crowded street. When you find yourself boxed in and confined by remnants and relics of an old life, reclaim the space like wild vines that devour buildings.

Hold a seed in your hand. It is small, dull, and pretty unassuming, but inside this fragile thing tossed about by the wind, there is a thriving potential. Pentacles represent the immense will to live and thrive. Cold, solid winter ground yields little fruit, but when the sun returns in spring and that unassuming seed is sown into her belly, a whole new world can begin.

Spinning on this big, blue ball in space, we are reminded that our Earth is older than anything we can imagine. She is hard and enduring, brutal and tenacious. She is soft, sandy, and ripe with paradise. Life and death meet in the womb of the earth. When Pentacles appear in your life, become aware of your journey, the proof of your experiences, the scars of your pain, and the strength you've found through time. Muster the courage to embrace your fertile nature and pull from the depths of your soul the seeds you wish to plant with your words, your actions, your love, and your attention.

When Pentacles cards appear, you're being quickened to life and reminded of your potential and power. You are awakening and returning to your true nature. This could be a time of ending so that something new can begin. Look for the fruits of your labor, the potential to create, or the power to regrow a new life. What are you bringing to life? What is your body telling you? How does your home make you feel? Are you prosperous or depleted? Are you struggling to get by or do you thrive?

Work with the earth by going outside to be in nature. Take a walk through the woods or a park. Find a tree or boulder to sit on and feel the stability of nature in action. Let your fears and hopes flow into the earth, root yourself deeply in this moment, and know you are ripe with potential. Ask the earth to show you all the ways you've already created what you want and need. Create or look for a natural talisman, like a stone, crystal, or some found object while in nature. Let this be a reminder that you are powerful.

As you explore the cards, be mindful of which element resonates with you and which element challenges you. What process or energy are you currently experiencing? What energy would better enrich your experience?

### JOURNALING EXERCISE

Create a page for each element. On each page, write down all the words that come to mind when you think of this element. For example, words such as *ground, planet, strength* may resonate for earth, while *fury, calm, breeze* may be words that conjure up the energy of air. Let whatever comes up, come. Do not judge. Just let the words flow.

Do this until you have a full page of words for each element.

These words may help you develop your own organic meanings for the elements.

# 6

# Healing with Tarot

You've met the Birth Card archetypes and learned how they can help you show up as the best version of you. You've learned about the elements as they figure into the Minor Arcana and how they can assist you. But life isn't so simple, is it? Even when we work to confront the dark spots within, life still has a way of throwing curveballs. It happens to all of us: loss, depression, divorce, addiction, family troubles, domestic violence. We may all face these things and more at one time or another. No one is immune from troubles.

Tarot can be an excellent tool for introspection. Use these Tarot spreads for reflection. As you lay the cards out, meditate on each image. What are the cards saying to you? What feelings do the questions and spreads invoke? What plans of action might you consider taking upon further reflection? These spreads aid you in looking within and finding space for healing.

Although in the Birth Cards section we looked only at the Major Arcana, for the spreads, please use the whole deck so you can get a complete picture, including the elements and associations of the Minor Arcana as well. Here are some keywords for each Tarot card that you can refer to as a jumping-off point.

## MAJOR ARCANA

*Fool—beginning, journey, start, faith, new, courage*

*Magician—talent, skill, willpower, manifest, awareness, power, empower*

*High Priestess—instincts, intuition, feminine wisdom, passivity, secrets, sacred*

*Empress—abundance, motherhood, creativity, pleasure, prosperity, feminine leadership, fertility, marriage, passion, sensuality*

*Emperor—security, power, rulership, paternal, authority, provider, stability, leader, boss*

*Hierophant—tradition, conformity, spiritual leadership, rules, order, teacher, mentor, student*

*Lovers—love, relationships, choices, higher guidance, compromise, teamwork, mediation*

*Chariot—willpower, direction, driver's seat, victory, control, lead, destination*

*Strength—power, gentleness, helper, conquer, soothe, heal*

*Hermit—wisdom, teacher, solitude, quiet, withdrawal, seeker, meditation*

*Wheel of Fortune—pivot, change, momentum, shift, luck, karma, dharma*

*Justice—karmic debt, law, decisions, fairness, rights, legal*

*Hanged Man—wait, faith, trust, sacrifice, perspective*

*Death—endings, beginnings, clearing, release, change, transformation*

*Temperance—compromise, mediation, balance, moderation, alchemy*

*Devil—bondage, addiction, stuck, oppression, fear, ignorance, materialism, negativity, abuse, shadow*

*Tower—release, upheaval, chaos, revolution, change, teardown*

*Star—healing, health, joy, positivity, hope, fame, visibility, authenticity*

*Moon—fear, anxiety, unseen, illusion, change, darkness*

*Sun—success, happiness, passion, joy, children, abundance*

*Judgment—rebirth, shedding, transition, change, endings, higher calling, awakening, woke*

*World—ending, completion, closure, success, graduation, achievement, goal, satisfaction*

## MINOR ARCANA

*Ace of Cups—love, opening, healing, beginning*

*Two of Cups—attraction, meeting, love, relationship*

*Three of Cups—joy, friendship, party, celebration*

*Four of Cups—frustration, disinterest, ennui, laziness*

*Five of Cups—sadness, grieving, surrendering, loss, sorrow*

*Six of Cups—past, home, security, nostalgia, wistfulness, yearning, children*

*Seven of Cups—decisions, dreams, fantasy, illusion*

*Eight of Cups—moving, leaving, seek, soul search, journey, travel*

*Nine of Cups—contentment, fulfillment, wish*

*Ten of Cups—family, security, children, celebration, success, fulfillment*

*Page of Cups—idealistic, sensitive young person, love note, new relationship*

*Knight of Cups—romantic partner, dreamer*

*Queen of Cups—nurturer, mother, caretaker, intuitive*

*King of Cups—kindly mature person, mastery of love*

*Ace of Wands—opportunity, creative venture, new leaf*

*Two of Wands—planning, dominion, success, vision*

*Three of Wands—expansion, travel, success, options*

*Four of Wands—joy, happiness, celebration, party, security*

*Five of Wands—conflict, game, sport, competition*

*Six of Wands—victory, success, tribe, leader, triumph, winning*

*Seven of Wands—confrontation, struggle, challenge, battle, overwhelm, fighting*

*Eight of Wands—trip, travel, news, progress, speed*

*Nine of Wands—anxiety, paranoia, setback, obstacles, wounded, beware*

*Ten of Wands—struggle, burden, overload, oppression, hardship, strain, hard labor*

*Page of Wands—bright student, creative offer*

*Knight of Wands—adventurous young person*

*Queen of Wands—inspiring, warm, creative fire*

*King of Wands—powerful, inspirational leader*

*Ace of Swords—mental stimulation, breakthrough, conflict, advance, carpe diem, new thought*

*Two of Swords—wait, meditation, options, consideration, reflection, inward, stagnancy, truce*

*Three of Swords—sorrow, divorce, grief, loss, heartache, betrayal*

*Four of Swords—contemplation, healing, recuperation, planning, peace*

*Five of Swords—deception, dirty pool, nastiness, pain, war, battle, betrayal, hurt*

*Six of Swords—transition, moving on, support, journey, potential*

*Seven of Swords—betrayal, stealth, cunning, deception, cheating, sneakiness*

*Eight of Swords—limitations, stuck, stranded, bound, blockages, restraint, blindness*

*Nine of Swords—stress, nightmares, sleepless, insomnia, worry, anxiety, fear*

*Ten of Swords—ending, new beginning, pain, treachery*

*Page of Swords—intelligent young person, important message*

*Knight of Swords—a person who brings drama*

*Queen of Swords—thought leader, truth teller*

*King of Swords—an academic, philosopher, thought leader*

*Ace of Pentacles—fortune, opportunity, chance, job, venture*

*Two of Pentacles—multitasking, managing, options, weighing*

*Three of Pentacles—skill, apprenticeship, plans, collaboration, reward, recognition*

*Four of Pentacles—security, greed, miserliness, stability, prosperity, possessiveness*

*Five of Pentacles—hardship, outsider, poverty, setback, codependent, injury, homelessness*

*Six of Pentacles—giving, charity, humanitarian, beggar, balance, philanthropy*

*Seven of Pentacles—pause, labor, ponder, growth*

*Eight of Pentacles—job, progress, skill, apprenticeship, learning, perfectionism, success*

*Nine of Pentacles—prosperity, security, material success, protection, wealth*

*Ten of Pentacles—family, legacy, wealth, growth, magic*

*Page of Pentacles—apt pupil, financial news*

*Knight of Pentacles—a reliable young person*

*Queen of Pentacles—caretaker, curator, Mother Earth*

*King of Pentacles—King Midas, goals manifested*

These are only keywords or prompts to get your intuition going. Trust your own interpretations! If the image says something else to you, let your own inner wisdom guide you to creating meanings that feel right for you and your situation.

Remember: your intuition knows what's up. Let it guide you!

## *Tarot as a Mirror to Your Inner World*

When you begin the journey of working with Tarot, you are embarking on an adventure of personal transformation. This book isn't specifically about reading Tarot, rather it's a guide to using Tarot to heal and empower yourself, but understanding how Tarot can work for you is essential.

The Tarot is a language and collection of symbols that decode the energetic space around you. Beyond that, the cards actually mirror something within you that you already know to be true on some level. This is the juicy, luscious magic of working with Tarot to heal yourself and excavate your purpose and power.

When you lay out the cards, regardless of why, first notice how they move you.

*What is your initial reaction to the image in front of you?*

*Are you attracted to the card?*

*Or are you repulsed by it?*

When something triggers you in a positive or negative way, there is more under the surface to be explored. With this deep and compassionate awareness, you can unwind the pain and the purpose coiled deep in your soul to begin living more intentionally and purposefully.

In a world bent on telling you who you should be, taking a holistic approach to life and Tarot can allow you to find your own true voice. Commit to your personal growth and transformation by going into the unknown to discover the light within you. If you learn anything from this book, it should be that you always have a choice in your life about how you respond to or interact with a situation. You do not have to be what the world and those around you define you as or tell you you ought to be.

All of us live on a spectrum between being in the flow of life and being in resistance. Acting in the flow means you are open, engaged, and abundant, and everything moves fluidly. You feel supported and expansive. It doesn't mean things are easy or light and fluffy. It means you are aware enough of what is happening to know when something hurts and when something feels good. That way you can pivot in a new direction.

When you are in resistance, you feel lost, blocked, and stuck on a loop. The chronic situations in your life are places that need attention and action. Breathe awareness into these painful places and ask: How can I grow from this?

There will always be areas in your life that are more challenging than others. Focusing completely on the good is not the way to grow your personal power. The other parts of your life that are in resistance will just continue to spiral out, which is why shadow work is such a key component of healing and transforming.

If you remain open and curious about life, even when things are sticky, you will learn to move with the tides, re-coordinate with the terrain, and locate your center. Being open, asking questions, and reflecting are the most nourishing things you can do. Awareness is the key to healing.

When you view the cards lying in front of you as a holographic representation of a situation, you can explore them more completely. Your initial response is going to be the first clue into how this energy is blocking or nourishing you and what you can gain from it.

Go deeper. Notice what catches your attention in the image. What is the mood of the card? Who or what appears on the image? Notice how these cards are working together or opposing each other. Are any of the characters facing toward or away from each other? Do you notice a theme among the images?

This is where the structure of the Tarot can help you understand the message more. If there is an abundance of one suit, ask yourself what that means in a symbolic or metaphoric way. If you were to draw all Wands, which are the element of fire, you might look at how you are lit up, inflamed, or engaged. What fuels the situation?

If you have all Major Arcana cards—the big mysteries—you might be working on a higher level or dealing with a situation that crosses into all the boundaries of your life.

Shaheen has found that the cards tend to unfold their message for him in a certain way:

"When I work with a card, I notice the whole image first. The initial impression can reveal ample amounts of information. Then I work my way into the image, scanning from top to bottom or left to right to see what draws my attention. Where your attention goes, the energy is flowing and making itself known. Your eye might be drawn to a particular color, like the warm yellow of the Sun card, so what does that mean for you? Or you might notice the little details such as the snail on the Nine of Pentacles. He is tiny and easy to miss, but what message might he hold for you?

Be patient with yourself as you move into each image. Trust yourself completely, and allow the cards to move you. If something calls to your attention, but you don't understand why, just trust it, write it down, and visit it later.

## *Inquiry Unlocks the Secret of the Tarot*

As you thumb through your deck of Tarot cards, you will find a whole circus of people, images, and experiences. Discovering each card can be exciting and a bit daunting, especially when you view them from your analytical self that wants to know everything right away. As you discover the cards' nuances, you will grow, and as you grow, the cards will grow with you. Let every time you see a card be like the first time and remain curious!

If you want to broaden your experience, begin each reading or session with intention. Know why you are consulting the deck and what you'd like to reveal. Asking a question is essential. The clearer the question is, the more in-depth the answer will be. Your question is your guiding light. It makes the information you discover in the cards relevant. Each question will change the meaning of the cards because you are looking at them through that lens.

Imagine if you went to a doctor or therapist because you had an issue. You wouldn't walk in and say, "Hey, something hurts somewhere. Can you figure out what it is?" You would begin with an intention to understand your pain and symptoms. You would start right where you are, with what you know, and then dig deeper into the issue. Tarot is the same way!

You will find a number of spreads to help you begin your process. As you work on one issue through the lens of your question and the spread you choose, you'll find there can be another question underneath that original query. Inquire deeper and find out more. Tarot can be an open conversation if you allow it.

Craft your question in a way that gives you power—power to pivot, change, or move forward. Be clear what and whom you're asking about.

Maybe you're grappling with a painful romantic relationship that's left you feeling depleted, depressed, and confused. Your first inclination might be to ask something like: What does this person feel about me? Or when will we get back together?

A question like this puts all the power in their hands or the hands of fate, when really you'd like to know: How can I move past my pain? Start there, and see where it goes.

Sometimes you might just see what comes up in the cards. That's okay to do, but consider this more as a contemplation exercise rather than a way to get specific answers. You can also look at different angles of the same situation or alternative paths that you could take. In this way, Tarot becomes a microscope to show you different parts and pieces making up the whole.

Here are a few sample questions:

*What do I need to know about this situation?*

*How can I move forward?*

*What will nourish me most?*

*What choices can I make here?*

*Why do I feel . . .?*

*What is the next step I can take?*

*How will I feel if . . .?*

*Where can I change directions?*

## *The Three Powers of Tarot*

Traditionally, Tarot is used as a tool to understand the trajectory of a situation. You might look to the past and the present to understand your current path and how that will unfold. Some people avoid making predictions because the future is a fluid space being created moment to moment, but it's easy to say if you are walking in a straight line, you'll eventually run into the wall up ahead.

The magic of Tarot really lies in its creative potential to explore different facets of a story and to see the possibilities that are present for you. Working with the cards in this way allows your practice to be fluid, nourishing, and creative. You begin to see how life can be for you, rather than just accepting it as it is. Remember, you want the Tarot to empower you!

1. Tarot is diagnostic. It shows you all the parts and pieces of the situation and how they are coming together to create this reality you are in right now. This is the first layer of a reading.

2. Tarot is retroactive. When you explore the facets of a reading, you'll find much of what you experience now is rooted in the past. Past pain, trauma, and experience shape who we are, what we believe, and how we move through the world. If you know where your past pain lies, you can choose images that evoke this past experience to safely interact with it. From there, you can change the story. You can deconstruct the story you already know to reframe it in a new light that empowers you. Remember, energy is fluid.

3. Tarot is creative. If Tarot can show you the possibilities of the future, then it can help you create the future. When you look at the future and what cards appear, you're seeing how your present energetic story is weaving together to create your path. If you clarify your desire into a clear intention, you can choose which images represent the new story you'd like to tell.

The potential of Tarot lies in your ability to dream, create, stretch, and pivot your point of view. The healing capabilities are endless when it comes to working with the cards. Each card is a mirror into your life and a doorway into a new way of life.

## How to Ask Good Questions

There is an art form to asking good Tarot questions. Questions such as "Will he come back?" or "Should I go for this job?" or other "yes/no" questions are passive in nature and imply that you have no role in your future. Although Tarot can indicate a likely outcome or best paths, it's better to seek out empowering information that puts the responsibility for your future in your own hands.

These guidelines are helpful for forming excellent Tarot questions:

Starting out a question with "what do I" or "how can I" will put you in a proactive position, and this will make your Tarot deck a trusted ally rather than some fortune-telling device. Here are a few sample questions:

*What do I need to know about ___________________?*

*What can I do to improve___________________?*

*What is the best way to _______________?*

*What am I not seeing about this situation at the moment?*

*Where would my energy be best spent in this situation?*

*How can I support __________?*

*What is my role in this situation?*

*What is the most powerful decision I can make when it comes to _____?*

Once you have a question or situation in mind, it's time to break out the cards and begin reading!

## How to Work with the Spreads

**You'll need:**

***Your favorite Tarot deck.*** *This book uses the Rider Waite Smith deck, but you may have another that you prefer. Feel free to use whatever deck speaks best to you!*

***Your journal.*** *Taking time to journal your answers will help you to embody the readings and connect to the cards more deeply. You may also find, upon further* *reflection, new answers and insights to add to your interpretation. Your journal can become a living, breathing, and healing manifesto!*

*Dedicate your journal to this healing and empowering journey. And know that your journal can look however you'd like. Write in it, draw in it, collage and paint in it. (Shaheen points out: When I feel really angry, I like to get big markers and write in bold letters, outside of the lines, across the page, upside down.) A journal is a mirror for self-reflection; it shows you where you are and where you can look from a new vantage point.*

**What to do:**

1. Page through this section and find a spread that speaks to you. Once you have decided which one you'd like to work with, find a quiet spot where you will not be disturbed. Shut the door, light some candles, or burn a little incense if you like. Treat this time as a sacred spiritual practice.

2. Take a minute to sit quietly and connect with your breath. Close your eyes and take a few nice, slow, and deep breaths.

3. You may want to say a short prayer, blessing, or invocation. Something as simple as "may these cards shed insight on what I need to know" or "may the answers I need arise" or "please allow me to connect with my higher guidance."

4. Shuffle the cards while concentrating on your question or situation. There is no wrong or right way to shuffle. Just do what feels natural and comfortable.

5. When you feel ready, put the deck on the table facedown and cut the cards into three piles. Put them back together any way you'd like.

6. You can take the cards from the top of the deck, or, if you prefer, fan the cards out and choose them based on your intuition for each position.

7. Take a minute to study the cards. What are the images saying to you? Trust your gut and write down your first impressions in your journal. Let the words spill from you! No filter, please. If you are drawing a blank, write down the name of the card and maybe a word or two that seem to describe the card. For example, for the Five of Wands you might write: fight, conflict, game. Later on, you can come back to this card and add more insights. Just allowing the images to speak to you will

help you access their message. Think of them like images in a storybook. What do you see? What is the tone or mood? What characters are at play? Let the colors, illustrations, and even the weather give you insight.

8. Once you are done journaling, sit quietly and study the images again. Read your words. Notice how you feel.

9. Before you end your session, you might take a photo of the spread so you have a record of the images. Sometimes going back to a spread to just see the way each card relates to one another can add another layer of insight. You can even use the spread like a healing mandala that crystallizes a particular energy you're working on.

A gentle reminder: While Tarot can be a lovely ally, it is in no way to be construed as or substituted for psychological counseling or any other type of therapy or medical advice. It is not meant to replace the care of licensed attorneys, business consultants, financial advisors, psychologists, or other health-care professionals.

## *The Spreads*

Look over the spreads and find one that is appropriate to your needs or appeals to you.

### Body Mind Spirit

The Body Mind Spirit spread is a classic and the perfect "check-in" Tarot spread. This is a quick way to see how you're doing—or where you need healing. The spread consists of three cards: one each for body, mind, and spirit.

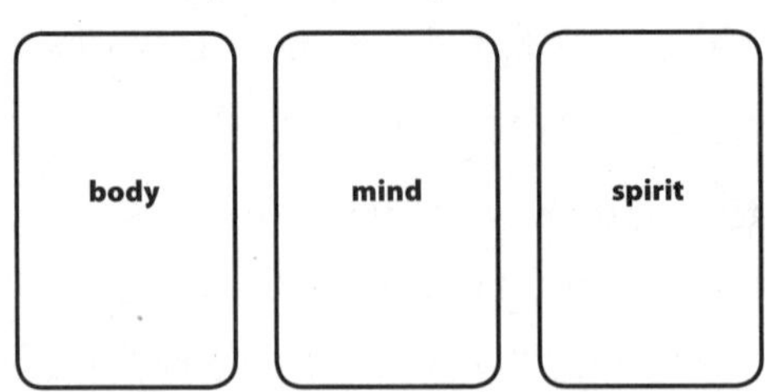


The Body Mind Spirit spread is a wonderful way to see your energetic story at work. You can disentangle the thoughts, beliefs, and feelings that could be holding you back to find a new stream of movement in your life.

Shuffle the deck and fan the cards out facedown. Let your intuition guide you as you pick cards for your body, mind, and spirit. Turn the cards over. What are they telling you about yourself in the present moment?

Here is an example of cards pulled by Sondra, a woman who recently lost her job and is looking for new work.

**Body:** *Sondra draws the Tower. The Tower symbolizes a shock to the system but also fear of change. Losing her job has created great anxiety for Sondra. She admits that it has kept her awake at night. This has also led to unhealthy habits—namely, eating her feelings. Sondra is aware that she needs to address her stress in a better way.*

**Mind:** *Sondra picks up the Ten of Wands. The Ten of Wands is the card of burdens and hard labor. Sondra is a single mother, so this period of unemployment is difficult for her and her family. She's feeling overwhelmed and like the whole weight of the world is resting on her shoulders. At times, she feels like giving up, but knows that she cannot.*

**Spirit:** *Sondra pulls the Knight of Cups. The Knight of Cups signals openness and love. Her spiritual life has always given her comfort in the past. Returning to her spiritual practices will help her to navigate this rough terrain. Sondra says she has recently joined a meditation group to ease her stress. The leader of the group has offered her helpful guidance. This is the one place where she feels safe at this time. She is making wise choices in this arena.*

This spread shows Sondra a need to take better care of herself. Also, the Ten of Wands is significant: this indicates that Sondra has taken on too much. Perhaps this may be a good time to check with her family and see if they can offer support until she is back on her feet.

## When You're Feeling Low

This simple two-card spread is good for those times when you're feeling down and looking for some inner guidance.

Here's how it works:

Flip through the deck, and consciously choose a card to represent how you're feeling at the moment. For example, if you're feeling sad, you might choose the Five of Cups. Anxious? Maybe the Nine of Swords or Nine of Wands. Look for an image that best illustrates your state of mind.

Now, shuffle the deck thoroughly. Fan it out facedown, and pull one card. This represents your solution or "Tarot prescription." Take time to reflect on the cards, and then journal your thoughts.

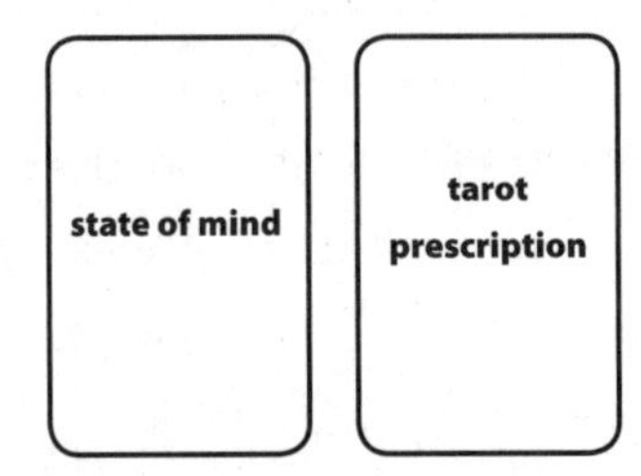


Brody has been feeling a bit lost since his divorce. Although he's moved on to a new relationship, the custody arrangement has made it hard for him to see his children as much as he'd like. Plus, he misses his ex. The card he has chosen to represent his feelings is the Three of Swords. The Tarot prescription he has pulled is the Hierophant.

The Hierophant can symbolize a counselor or mediator. In this case, Brody feels that perhaps he needs to explore working with a therapist to heal the wounds left from the divorce. But he also sees this as advice to seek a legal mediator to work out a better arrangement with his ex. Although there are no guarantees that this will lead to an improvement in the situation, it's a step in the right direction with his children.

## The Grief Spread

At some point in your life, you will deal with a loss. Everybody does. But everybody expresses grief differently. Some people show it outwardly, while others are private. And some people seem to move on quickly, while others may hold on indefinitely. Although the grieving process is unique, every person can benefit from reflection. This spread is based on the Five Stages of Grief, a framework created by Elisabeth Kübler-Ross and David Kessler in their groundbreaking book *On Grief and Grieving*. Use this spread as a way to contemplate on and work with your loss.

Shuffle the cards and place them facedown. Cut the deck into five piles. Choose one card from the top of each pile for these questions:

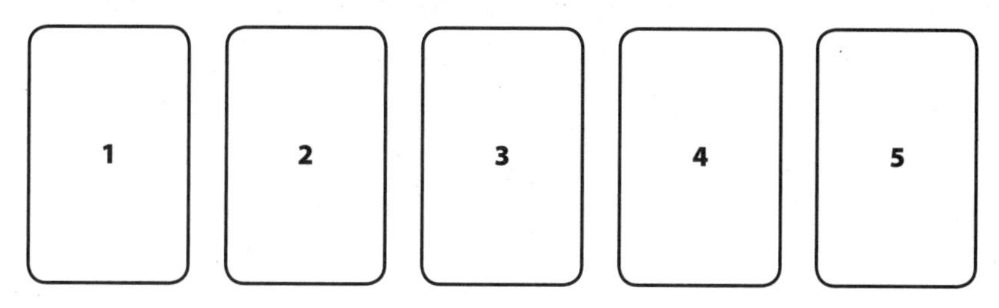


*Card 1. What do I need to look at right now?*

*Card 2. What can I learn from my anger?*

*Card 3. What can I do to find peace with the present moment?*

*Card 4. What is my sadness trying to tell me?*

*Card 5. What do I need to accept at this time?*

Trista lost her son a few years ago through violence. She's never been able to move forward, even though her family has told her it's "time to let him go." As she says, "How do you let go when your child is murdered?"

She chooses the Grief Spread to try to understand how she's feeling and what she might need to know in order to heal.

**What do I need to look at right now?** *Trista draws the Star. The Star symbolizes hope and inspiration, which means Trista may want to look at how her loss might serve as a way to inspire others. She has been moved to speak out* *against gun violence in her neighborhood, something she might have never done if it weren't for her loss. While she can't deny that her tragedy has been painful, it's also given her an opportunity to shine a light on positivity and healing.*

**What can I learn from my anger?** *Trista pulls the Magician reversed. Anger and willpower, when misdirected, can lead to more violence. But taking that anger and employing it properly can turn it into something that creates change. Anger is an energy, and Trista may find that her anger over the loss of her son can be best applied to create change in the world instead of holding it in and feeling hate for the people who murdered him.*

**What can I do to find peace with the present moment?** *Trista's card is the Page of Wands. Pages are messengers and the Page of Wands is the fiery messenger because of the association of Wands with the fire element. There is a strong vibe between all the cards so far that shows Trista has an opportunity to do something powerful in her community. Take that fire and use it to inspire others! Encourage children to make a change and put down their arms. This is a productive and dynamic way to create peace. Because the Page is also a symbol of a new beginning, this may be urging Trista to start working with youth in some way—perhaps speaking at schools.*

**What is my sadness trying to tell me?** *Trista draws the King of Wands. This is telling her, "Use it as fuel." Sadness, like anger, can be a motivator. The King of Wands takes energy and does something big with it. Again, the cards seem to be encouraging Trista to step into a leadership role.*

**What do I need to accept at this time?** *Trista's final card is the Three of Swords. This is a hard card to see and a painful reminder that no matter what—even through conscious leadership—her son cannot be brought back. He's gone and nothing will ever replace her child. This is a difficult cross for a mother to bear, but unfortunately, Trista must carry it. It's also a sign that she may have to accept that she will still feel sad and mad—perhaps for the rest of her life.*

## Tarot for Addiction

"I've tried to quit, but it's like I'm hardwired to fail. I feel like I'm hitting bottom, but I don't know what comes next. I'm terrified I'm going to relapse."

Addiction is a mental, physical, and spiritual affliction—and when your mind, body, and soul are tangled up in chemicals, anxiety, and obsessive thoughts, it can be damn near impossible to make confident, life-affirming choices.

If you're struggling with addiction, these spreads will help you to find your way from rock bottom to radiance.

### TWELVE STEPS TO FREEDOM SPREAD

Most people are familiar with the Twelve Steps popularized by Alcoholics Anonymous. This spread uses some of those concepts as a tool for reflection.

Shuffle the cards and fan them out facedown. Choose one card for each question. Reflect on the Tarot images and then write your thoughts in your journal.

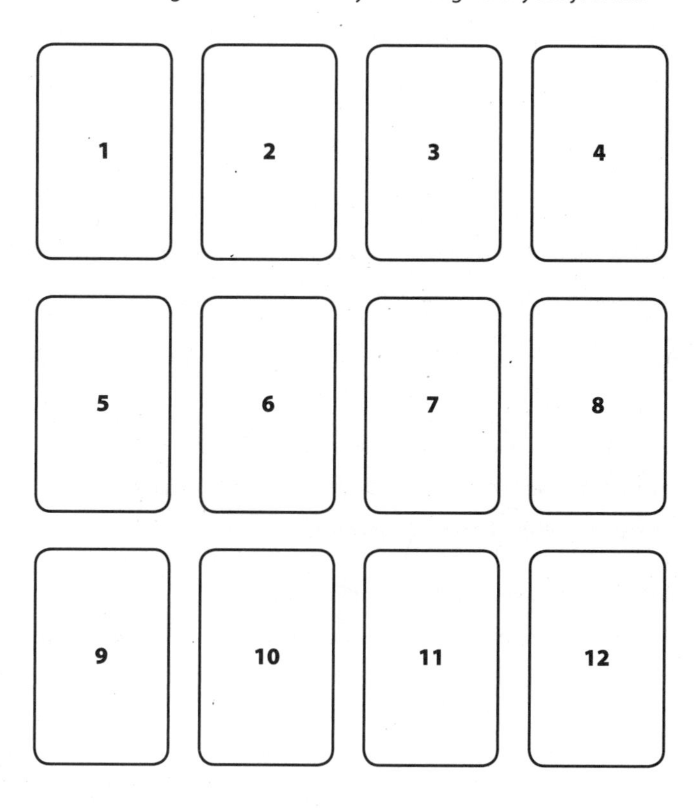

*Card 1. When do you feel powerless?*

*Card 2. What do you believe about yourself?*

*Card 3. What decision can you make right now to turn things around?*

*Card 4. When you look in the mirror, what do you see?*

*Card 5. What wrongs do you need to face right now?*

*Card 6. What is one thing you can take responsibility for right now?*

*Card 7. Name one way you are powerful, whole, and strong.*

*Card 8. How might you make amends to people you've harmed through your addiction?*

*Card 9. Where do you need to forgive yourself?*

*Card 10. What do you want to admit right now?*

*Card 11. What does your higher self want you to know right now?*

*Card 12. What can you commit to in the next thirty days?*

Elizabeth has been struggling with alcohol for years. It has created havoc in her family and strained her relationships with her daughters. She's been working on her sobriety for a few months. After journaling around the questions, she shares her thoughts:

**When do you feel powerless?** *Elizabeth draws the Knight of Wands. When there is a crisis and I'm expected to rescue others, I feel downright out of my element. I know I should be doing more to help my loved ones, but I am so busy trying to get my own life under control that I feel I have nothing else left to give. When other people need my help, I am powerless.*

**What do you believe about yourself?** *Elizabeth pulls the King of Wands. Somewhere deep down inside, I see a person who is brave and courageous. Even though I may not act like this in my real life, it's how I know I am at the core.*

**What decision can you make right now to turn things around?** *Elizabeth gets the Seven of Cups. This card makes me think of sitting at a bar and trying to choose which drink to have! I guess I can decide to avoid bars or situations where alcohol is present. That way, I don't have to think about it.*

**When you look in the mirror, what do you see?** *Elizabeth picks up the Ace of Swords. I see someone at the beginning of a breakthrough. There are still mountains to cross, but I'm finding the tools I need to be victorious.*

**What wrongs do you need to face right now?** *Elizabeth draws the Emperor reversed. I know that the Emperor is concerned with security. I know that my actions and choices have undermined my family's sense of stability. I need to start fixing that first and foremost.*

**What is one thing you can take responsibility for right now?** *Elizabeth gets the Four of Cups. I can say no. It may seem like a simple thing, but it's not.*

**Name one way you are powerful, whole, and strong.** *Elizabeth pulls the Nine of Cups. I can find contentment, even in small things.*

**How might you make amends to people you've harmed through your addiction?** *Elizabeth draws the Hanged Man. By making sacrifices for them, namely giving up my drinking once and for all, and also not playing the martyr. I have often taken on that role as an excuse to drink.*

**Where do you need to forgive yourself?** *Elizabeth gets the Page of Cups. I have a lot of guilt around my children. I know that, even though I've let them down at times, I've also been a loving parent. I need to remember that—and forgive myself for those periods when I wasn't there for them in the way they needed me most.*

**What do you want to admit right now?** *Elizabeth sees the Three of Cups. I admit that I enjoyed the social part of drinking. In fact, it allowed me to let down my inhibitions and be the "life of the party." I guess there is a part of me that recognizes that drinking made me think I was being fun, when the truth is, I was only avoiding things that I needed to face.*

**What does your higher self want you to know right now?** *Elizabeth pulls the King of Swords. My higher self wants me to know that I can master my sobriety. I have everything I need to transform my relationship with alcohol—and with my life. I also suspect my higher self is reminding me that I need to be honest with myself. Even going through these questions, I feel that perhaps I am glossing over some things because there are still some truths I am not ready to face. Whoa. I have a lot more work ahead of me.*

**What can you commit to in the next thirty days?** *Elizabeth looks at the Five of Pentacles. I can commit to addressing the codependence issues that are at the heart of my problem. I am currently working on this with my sobriety coach, and it's something I need to delve into more deeply.*

## WHEN YOU'VE RELAPSED

The road to recovery is often paved with relapses. Studies suggest that about 70–90 percent of individuals experience a slipup. Many addicts will relapse more than once before they finally get sober. It's part of the recovery process, and there is no reason to be ashamed if it happens to you.

Relapse is not an indication of failure—it's a sign that more work and support are needed. If you've experienced a relapse, this three-card spread will help you to reflect on what led up to it and what your next steps need to be.

Shuffle the deck, and cut it into three piles. Take one card from the top of each pile, and use these questions as prompts.

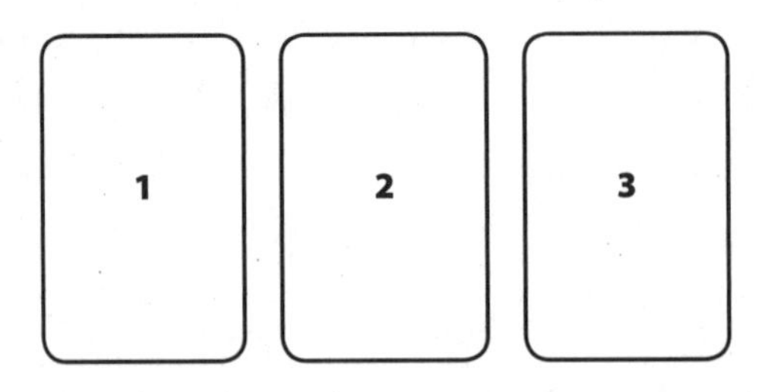


*Card 1. What do I need to know about the root of this relapse?*

*Card 2. What lessons can I take away from this experience?*

*Card 3. What is the next step I need to take in order to get back on track?*

After a back injury, Mike became addicted to painkillers. He successfully completed an inpatient program at a local clinic but relapsed three months later. He's ready to reenter an outpatient treatment and wants to explore the relapse in order to understand what triggered this and what he may need to do differently. Mike has journaled around the questions and shares his thoughts:

> **What do I need to know about the root of this relapse?** *Mike draws the Seven of Pentacles reversed. Although I received an excellent plan from the outpatient program, I stopped following it. I got bored with the daily meditations and group meetings. Plus, life got busy. Work picked up, and I started slacking on my sobriety and self-care. It didn't take long before I started feeling like crap, which meant I started looking for relief. That's what has led me to where I am now.*
>
> **What lessons can I take away from this experience?** *Mike pulls the Hierophant. This is a sign that I need to stick with the program and seek professional counseling again. I thought I was ready to be off on my own, but I guess I wasn't. I feel a bit ashamed that I couldn't just do this by myself. But rather than letting that get me down, I am going to swallow my pride and admit I need more help.*
>
> **What is the next step I need to take in order to get back on track?** *Mike gets the Five of Wands. I need to get in and fight this with all my might! What's interesting to me in this card is there are a bunch of other guys fighting too; it's another sign that I need to be working with others who are fighting this disease rather than going it alone. I'm going to recommit to my therapy and group meetings. This might help me get on track and stay on track.*

## WHEN YOUR LOVED ONE IS AN ADDICT

Substance abuse doesn't affect just the addict. It also impacts their loved ones. This can range from financial issues to physical or emotional problems. Codependence can deepen the cycle of addiction, which can take the family down a dark, draining path.

Although each situation is different, the effects of living with an addicted family member can lead to guilt, anxiety, fear, and feelings of helplessness. How can you be there for your loved one while still maintaining healthy boundaries?

Theresa had a longtime friend who struggled with heroin addiction for many years. Dave had been in and out of rehab and jail, which would often lead to stretches when he'd be clean. She explains the impact this relationship has had on her:

// We lost touch for a couple of years, and during that time, he sank deeper into this addiction. When we resumed contact, he was homeless and in terrible shape. We tried to help him, but our attempts to give him support were wasted. The money we pressed into his palms went straight up his arm. At wits' end, we finally decided to stop enabling him, which meant putting up strong boundaries and no more handouts. He called a few times, looking for help, but we knew he was using again so we ignored those calls. A few days went by, and we got the news: he had died of an overdose. Although I knew that we had to create a bottom line, I am still haunted to this day. I often wonder if I could have done anything different or better. But the truth is probably not. Addiction is a hard taskmaster for both the addict and the people who love them. Whether a loved one is in the midst of their addiction or at the tail end of recovery, family and friends also need time to heal too.

This spread is good for finding your strength to support your addicted family member, whether they are in active addiction or on the road to recovery.

Shuffle the cards, and focus on your loved one. Cut the deck into three piles, and then put the deck back together. Pulling from the top of the deck, lay out the cards in two rows of three. The first row symbolizes the addict. The second row symbolizes you.

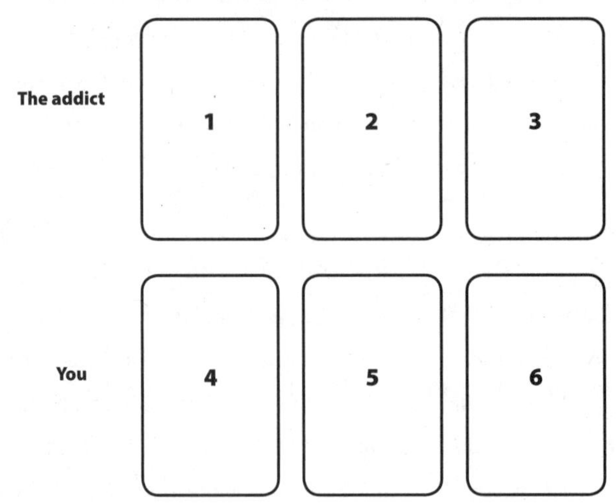

The three cards for the addict are as follows:

*Card 1. What do I need to know about ________'s current state?*

*Card 2. What does ____________ need at this time?*

*Card 3. What do I need from ___________ at this time?*

The three cards for you are as follows:

*Card 4. What boundaries do I need to set now?*

*Card 5. What support can I offer now?*

*Card 6. What do I need to do for myself at this time?*

Charlie's mother, Jane, has been an opioid addict for many years. She has gone through rehab many times, often staying clean for years. She's currently using, so he has decided to set clear boundaries with her, which means she is no longer allowed at his house. He wants to explore how to help her and love her while still keeping his own life drama-free.

Here are his cards and his interpretations:

**What do I need to know about Jane's current state?** *Charlie pulls the Three of Cups. For her, this relapse seems to be due to her social life. When she's with her friends, she wants to party. She does not seem to be taking this seriously. In fact, she says she is only doing it on the weekends. I know this is going to lead to bigger problems down the road because there is no such thing as "only doing it a little" when you have an addiction issue.*

**What does Jane need at this time?** *Charlie draws the Eight of Cups. I'm not sure how to interpret this. Does she need to go off on her own? Does she need me to walk away? This is a journey and we're both on it, but I am unsure of who needs to walk.*

**What do I need from Jane at this time?** *Charlie picks up the Two of Cups. Sigh. It's love, compromise, cooperation. I need her to be there for me and to meet me halfway. I don't know if that will happen, but yes, I wish my mother could put the pipe down and be the mother that I know is capable of being loving and present.*

**What boundaries do I need to set now?** *Charlie gets the Six of Pentacles. This is so clear to me: boundaries around money. This has been an ongoing issue. While I don't want to see her homeless or in trouble, I can't keep bailing her out like I did during her previous relapse. I need to set strict boundaries around financial support.*

**What support can I offer now?** *Charlie draws the Ten of Pentacles. It's interesting to see this card. I don't want to allow her in my house any longer due to issues around theft, but perhaps there may be some ways to allow her to be around my family. The elder in this card sits right outside the family scene. He's able to pet the dogs. This says to me that controlled time spent with the family will allow her to feel like she's not on the outside, but her theft will not be tolerated.*

**What do I need to do for myself at this time?** *Charlie pulls the King of Cups. This card indicates that I need to do a lot more work around my emotions at this time. I'm very torn because I love her so much, but I cannot keep living like this. I'm currently working with my therapist around loving myself but also loving her as she is. It's not easy and will be a lifetime of work due to the long-term addiction issue. Even if she gets clean permanently, these scars run deep.*

## Moving On

When a relationship comes to a crashing halt, it can be devastating. Hopes and dreams for the future dissipate, leaving only sadness in their wake. It can be tempting to hang on to the relationship and pine away for the past, even if it was rife with problems. That's because we often gloss over the hard stuff and remember only how we felt when the relationship was going well.

For Tarot readers, one of the most common questions is "will my partner come back?" This question is unhealthy. It keeps the querent trapped in an old story, sitting around waiting for something to happen. Often, when the cards show the person isn't returning, the questioner will get angry at the Tarot reader and search out someone who will feed the obsession instead. This keeps the cycle going and leaves the querent stuck longing for someone who probably has already moved on.

If you've experienced a split, resist the urge to ask this question. It will not serve your highest good. Keep in mind that even if your ex returns, there is often a great deal of work that would need to be done to heal the pain. Instead of focusing on them, it's better to put your energy into your own life. When you put your attention on you, you're taking responsibility for your own happiness, rather than leaving that job in the hands of your ex . . . or a Tarot reader.

This simple spread will help you to reflect on why you're holding on and uncover the next steps to take so that you can move forward.

Shuffle the cards and fan them out facedown. Choose one card for each question:

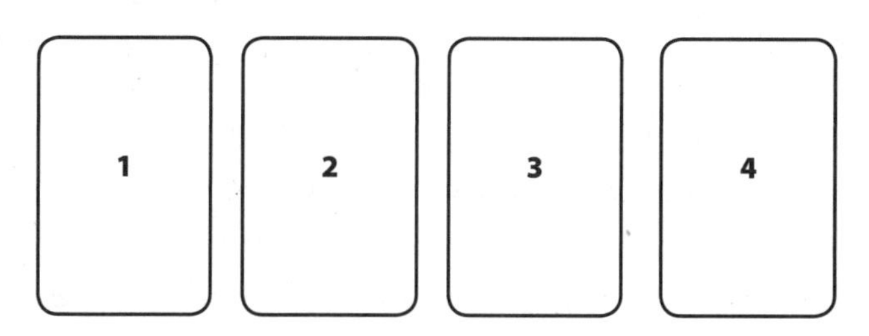


*Card 1. Why am I missing this relationship?*

*Card 2. Why am I holding on to this relationship?*

*Card 3. What do I need to see that I'm not at this time?*

*Card 4. What is my next step to let go and move on?*

Diana has been hanging on to her ex, Rod. It's been two years since they broke up, and he's in another relationship. She hopes that he will one day return to her, but she's also seeing the writing on the wall: he has had no contact with her and seems disinterested in resuming the relationship.

These are the cards she draws and her answers:

**Why am I missing this relationship?** *Diana picks up the Seven of Pentacles. I'm not sure what this card could mean. Am I missing the financial stability? Or maybe it's the fact that I felt that I could lean on him in hard times. We went through a lot together, and it was nice having his support.*

**Why am I holding on to this relationship?** *Diana draws the Eight of Wands. There have been opportunities to move on, but none of the men I have met have had the same passionate connection. Some of them wanted to move too fast for me; others seemed to lack that something that Rod and I shared. I wonder if there* *are no other men out there that might have the same passion. Frankly, I think there is a sexual reason, too, that makes me long for Rod.*

**What do I need to see that I'm not at this time?** *Diana pulls the Four of Cups. Because I am so hung up on him, I am not seeing any good options, even though there are probably some decent men around me. Instead, I'm comparing them all to him and assuming they are all boring. I have to admit that Rod and I fought . . . a lot. Some of these guys are "nice guys," and maybe I'm assuming that nice equals dull.*

**What is my next step to let go and move on?** *Diana picks up the Five of Swords. This card seems to say: Admit defeat. It's over. There are three people on this card—a sign that someone else is in the picture and he's probably not going to return to me. Perhaps it is time for me to realize that this is a done deal, whether I like it or not. I need to stop lying to myself about this, as hard as it may be.*

## When You Feel Lost

There may be times in your life when you feel adrift. Instead of charting a steady course, you're floating about with no sense of direction. This can be frustrating! But it doesn't have to be. This spread is perfect for reorienting yourself.

### THE COMPASS SPREAD

Shuffle the deck thoroughly. Once you feel ready, put it down, and cut it into four piles with your left hand.

You will be laying the cards out for the directions on a compass: north, south, east, and west. Take the first card off the top of the first pile. This will be south. Take the top card from the second pile. This will be west. The card from the third pile will be east, and the top card from the last pile is north.

The positions line up as follows:

*South: where you're coming from*

*West: what is directly behind you*

*East: what lies in front of you*

*North: the next move to make*

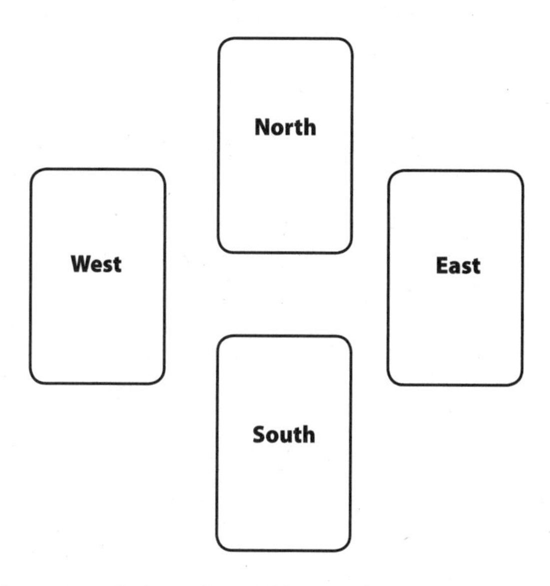


Theresa describes a time she's employed this spread:

> Recently, I found myself feeling a bit preoccupied with a certain aspect of my work. Instead of feeling excited about this particular offering, I had a sense that something was off. I chose the Compass Spread to help me sort it out.
>
> **South:** *Theresa gets the Hanged Man. Although the Hanged Man has an element of waiting to it, it can also symbolize being in limbo. This perfectly describes how I was feeling. Although the position I was in made me feel off, I was also having trouble letting go. In a way, I created the perfect storm for myself: instead of honoring my feelings, I had put this issue on hold and didn't deal with it . . . or how I felt.*
>
> **West:** *Theresa draws the Eight of Wands. New things started to come into my world. These were things that made me feel excited! But the energy here shows me that I can't move forward if I'm still bogged down by the very thing that is making me feel hamstrung.*
>
> **East:** *Theresa picks up the Eight of Cups. Here, the figure is walking away. That's it. There is no muss, no fuss. This simple card seemed to be saying: you're going to gather the courage to leave. It seemed to be telling me: you need to go, and you know it.*

**North:** *Theresa's last card is the Six of Pentacles. My next move is to put my time and energy into the things that people want, but those that still keep me feeling balanced. The work that I wanted to abandon for so long was depleting me. The new work that was trying to come to me looked like it would be an equal exchange of energy. Therefore, it would be wise for me to not only walk away from the work that didn't feed my soul but instead put my energy into the work that would.*

## When You're Struggling to Make a Decision

The Choices Spread is a quick way to look at your options when you find yourself needing to make a decision but can't see which way to go.

Here's what you do: Shuffle the cards, and when you feel ready, cut the deck and then put the cards back together. Fan the deck out, and choose one card for each option you are considering. Keep it simple—you don't want to have so many cards that you overwhelm yourself. Instead, try to limit your decision to no more than three options. Pick one more card for advice.

Here's how this spread might look:

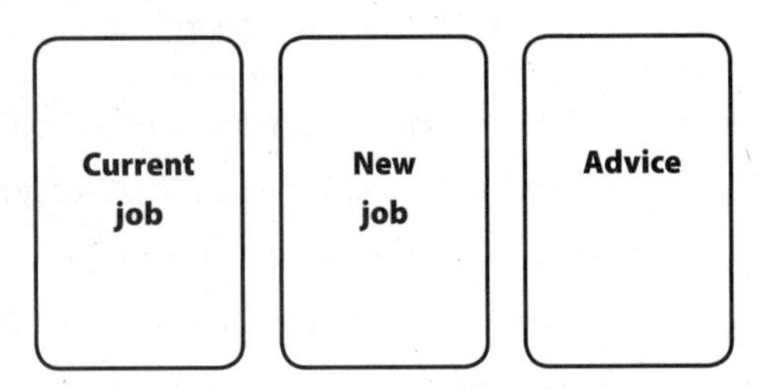


José is frustrated with his job. His boss is a jerk, and it's been a long time since he had a raise. Although he knows it's time to look for a job, he's nervous because the economy is struggling, and this job, although far from perfect, is stable and offers some benefits. Recently, his friend alerted him to an opening at his company. It sounds like it might be an option, but José wants to explore it a bit first.

Here are the cards José draws:

**Current job:** *José picks up the Five of Wands. This is the card of struggle and conflict, which indicates that should he stay in this job, he can probably expect more of the same. He'll need to be prepared to fight the powers that be, which means his stress levels will probably remain high.*

**New job:** *José pulls the Nine of Cups. This is the classic wish card, a sign that the offer his friend is talking about might meet his needs and then some. More importantly, this card shows happiness. Instead of the conflict of the Five of Wands, this card says he'll be sitting pretty.*

**Advice:** *José draws the Chariot. This is telling him go! It is as simple as that. Don't look back. Grab this opportunity and move on. This is the vehicle José has been waiting for.*

## *Creating Your Own Spreads*

Although we've provided a smattering of Tarot readings for different situations, there may be something on your mind that isn't addressed here. Perhaps you have a situation that is troubling you and you need a custom spread. Fortunately, that is easy to come up with.

The simplest way to create a spread is to meditate on the situation and the questions you'd like to ask. From there, jot your questions down. Each question will now become part of your spread.

For example, let's say you are in a toxic relationship and thinking of leaving, but you're not sure this is the right time because your finances are entangled. If you're seeking guidance on a situation like that, you may have questions such as:

*Card 1. What do I need to know about my relationship with my partner?*

*Card 2. What is the best step for me at this time?*

*Card 3. How might I protect my finances if I decide to move on?*

*Card 4. What is the best way to take care of myself going forward?*

Boom—you've got a simple four-card Tarot spread!

Let's look at an example. Linda is using our sample spread. Here are her answers:

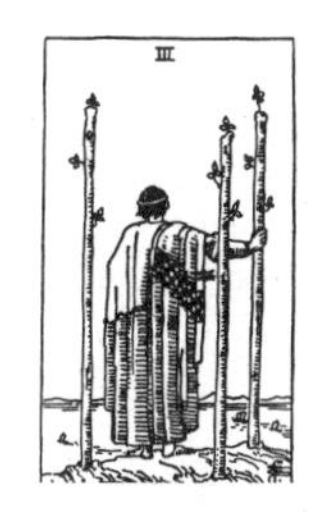

**What do I need to know about my relationship with my partner?** *Linda picks up the Six of Swords. We've survived some rocky times and seem to be moving forward, but the card looks sad. This is a symbol of a relationship that may be heading into a calmer time, but the damage is done.*

**What is the best step for me at this time?** *Linda gets the Ace of Pentacles, which lets her know that seeking financial independence may be her next move. If I have that, I would not feel so trapped! This may be the right time for me to invest my time and energy into getting a better job or creating a new budget. Seeking financial advice or assistance from an expert may also help me to craft a solid plan.*

**How might I protect my finances if I decide to move on?** *Linda pulls the Three of Wands. There is a planning element in this card, which coincides beautifully with the Ace of Pentacles. This might be the right time for me to seek guidance. If I have someone else looking out for my best interests, especially a financial advisor, I may be able to get on top of this situation and start planning for my future. Of course, this is also a reminder that I need to see where I can put money aside to prepare for my exit.*

**What is the best way to take care of myself going forward?** *Linda picks up the Knight of Pentacles. It seems that this is all about financial security. The truth is, if I weren't in a financial bind with my partner, I would have been gone long ago. This is a sure sign that the best thing I can do is get my financial independence from this situation. Once I have that, or at the very least a plan, I can start building a solid life on my own.*

## *Once You've Completed a Tarot Reading*

Once the reading is done, it's important to set it aside and go on with your life. Resist the urge to keep hammering the question or situation until you get the answer you want. That is rarely productive and often leads to mixed answers.

Still, there are a few good questions to ask yourself once you've completed the reading:

*How can I use this information?*

*What is one actionable step I can take to move forward?*

Reflect on these questions. Journal your answers. And then begin taking action toward the life you want. Your future is always in your hands. Make brave, excellent decisions going forward. If you don't like where your life is or what the cards are showing, you can change that. You're the boss.

# 7

# Believe in Magic

When life seems dark, you need to bring in the light. It's time for magic.

If you think that magic is only for witches or other mystical folks, hear this: you are magic. You are made of energy. That means you have the resources within yourself to reach your highest potential.

Magical rituals can help you do this. A ritual is a ceremony or sequence of actions that, when performed in the prescribed order, brings about a change. Rituals can be elaborate and full of many moving parts or simple. In most cases, simple is best.

## *What Is Magic?*

You came to this world to create, to express, and to thrive. If you think of life as art, the way you live becomes your expression of that art. The more fully you live, the more consciously you create, and the more intently you live, the more expressive and expansive you become. For many of us, finding our power and purpose can be a lifelong battle. We live in a society that is diligent in keeping us small and in our "place."

What you desire and what you deserve can seem like two very different things—especially when faced with so much manipulation, judgment, and oppression in the world. Some of us avoid our desires because we don't feel like we have a right to them. Other people avoid their desires out of fear of what comes from having them fulfilled.

For example, money is one of those sticky areas for a lot of people. Money is one of the many things that keep our world going around. Though it is a necessity in many ways, the *desire* for more money has a darker connotation. You'll hear many people say that money is "the root of all evil" or "it's a necessary evil." However, money is simply an object imbued with meaning and intention. Your relationship with money could be very different from my relationship with money. There is no right or wrong here; it's just a matter of belief supported by personal proof.

If you see greedy people with lots of money, you might fear that money will make you greedy. If you see hateful people with money, you might fear that money will make you hateful. If those are the beliefs you have around money, then you might avoid the desire to have more money altogether. In reality, your desire is to have what money can bring, not the inherent attitude or traits of a select few people with money. Look for a different set of proofs that money is good.

If the desire for money—or anything else for that matter—is backed by intention, then intention becomes the driving force for creating, having, and keeping what you want. Intentional living is the foundation of wellness and self-expression. In order to fulfill your purpose, you must acknowledge your desires, know that you deserve to have those desires, and that having those desires will only mean and bring whatever you decide to do with them—your intention.

Knowing that you deserve to have whatever you desire, if that desire is rooted in your well-being, allows you to be expansive. Like the trees desire the sun and the rain, you can desire love, happiness, abundance, and purpose, because what we really want is to be expressive, expansive, and whole and the things that allow each and every one of us to do that are abundant in the universe. We should all have them!

A self-expressed person is someone rooted in their own soul's wisdom and magic. If more people believed they deserved to have their desires expressed, we would live in an abundant, fluid world where everyone has what they need. It doesn't matter how many trees or flowers are drinking up sunshine because the sun shines regardless. Nature has an intention to grow, thrive, and express exactly what it is, and all the resources to do that are there for the taking.

What if we adopted that idea? How would things change?

That is the foundation of magic! Magic is the innate force inside of you seeking expression and communing with all things to truly unfurl and blossom into the world. When you ignite your desires with your intention and take action upon them, you become a cosmic magnet pulling to you all the things you desire or all the things required for you to live that desire and expression.

When you have an intention, you are being clear about what you want. Where most of us get confused is seeing our desire as a thing, when really our desire is a feeling. We desire *money* because we want to feel *abundant*.

Intention comes from the Latin word *intentio,* which means "stretching" or "purpose." To create magic in your life, you must crystallize your desire with an intention that has purpose and stretches you beyond what you already have or know. Whether or not you use intention, you are always creating your reality based on what you believe. Your belief shapes, pulls, and moves the energy or vibrations in the universe to support and expand your beliefs. You are always creating magic. The question is: are you creating magic that supports your highest good?

By nature, we are creative beings. Something is always pouring out of us and pulling in more of the same. The sad truth is that most of us walk through this world unaware or feeling undeserving of our desires, so we are creating more of the same limiting experiences, making life a chronic cycle of pain and unfulfillment. When you live from this place, you are basically generating a world based on someone else's truth.

Have you ever heard the expression "Never take advice from people who aren't where you'd like to be"? So why would you create a life around beliefs that don't feel right to your soul?

The beauty of discovering your magic is that you can begin changing at this very moment. When you choose to become intentional, your life begins to move in small ways that grow into big shifts. There is no guilt or shame in this because your pain shows you the path forward to finding your purpose. Pain and fear let us know where something isn't working. They indicate for us where we are playing small and outgrowing our boundaries. You stay in pain when you choose not to change.

Magic is your innate ability to create whatever you desire, and your purpose is to express whatever desire you have. However, what that looks like is up to you. You find it when you begin listening to how you feel and acting upon those feelings in clear intentional ways. This is a never-ending process. You don't get to that place of purpose and just stop, because you are a creative being expressing and expanding into infinity. Once you've grown into one expression, you begin evolving into something else.

Tarot offers you infinite and profound ways to become congruent and coherent about your life, your desires, and your spiritual nature. You have ample opportunities to heal and reveal the different parts of yourself and the different aspects of your nature. From there, you can make magic in your life!

Reading Tarot is magic in itself because it starts the alchemical process of change. When you inquire within and reveal insight, you begin to shift your energy, and that rewrites your story. Magic is the process of effecting change through vibration, so anything that shifts your vibration is magic.

Magic can be anything, from listening to music, reading Tarot, or going for a walk to actually working with ceremony, spellwork, and ritual. *Tarot for Troubled Times* is about magical living, and yet there are even more intentional ways to do magic.

## *How Do You Create Magic?*

Creating magic begins with your intention. If you know what you desire, you can do specific things that energetically affirm and draw to you more of those same experiences.

Think about magic like planting a garden. You know you want a luscious garden filled with colorful blooms and intoxicating scents. Your desire is to experience in reality the abundance of a beautiful, natural space. The next step is to find what that looks like and the tools and materials you need to bring it all to life. You must till the ground, nourish the soil, plant the seed, and give it time to grow.

Working magic is the same way! You must make yourself fertile to plant these new seeds of intention where they can bloom into your life.

When you do magic, you must make an agreement on all levels—mentally, physically, emotionally, and spiritually—that you can and will have what you want. Then you get to work! You look for the tools to create change in a way that feels comfortable to you. Just like all gardens can be different, so can all ways of doing magic.

You can create magic in so many different ways—from lighting candles to ignite your desires to inscribing talismans and sigils to attract or repel what you want, or simply using affirmations and spoken words to weave change.

You are the artist using your magic to express your art!

We have provided a number of spells, ceremonies, techniques, and exercises for you to employ to create magic in your life. Try them all to see what works best for you, but ultimately how you do magic is completely personal. Don't be afraid to explore and experiment. Draw upon the Tarot cards' images and elements to get ideas and direction for crafting your own spells and ceremonies.

## *Who Can Do Magic and What Can Magic Be Done For?*

Magic is for everyone. It isn't a religious path, though it can be part of one. Each and every religion has its own form of magic: magic is for the people to interface with their own creative force and the creative unknown of the universe. Whatever religious path you follow, you can do magic.

What you do magic for can change depending on your own personal beliefs. We would never advocate harming someone or taking something that isn't yours. Since we live in an abundant universe, there is no need for you to do that. If you desire money and work magic to get more money, then you can draw that money and abundance from anywhere in the universe.... There's no need to work magic on your rich aunt or anything manipulative.

With that being said, magic can be worked for anything: love, abundance, health, and well-being. Whatever that looks like for you, you can work magic for it.

## *How to Do Candle Magic*

Fire has a magical intensity that is unexplainable. We are fascinated by the glow of a candle, the crackling of a campfire, or a distant star burning brightly in the sky. Candle gazing can lull you into a trance. The flame dancing gracefully on the wick is breathing with life and power, warming and awakening something deep in your core.

Candle magic is one of the oldest forms of energy work, spanning time and tradition. Fire is one of the four elements of creation and holds the energy of transmutation, regeneration, and raw potential. For this reason, we light candles to ignite our prayers and intentions, to give life to our desires, and to burn up or transform negative energy in our lives into positive potential.

Shaheen describes how he works with candles:

> **//** I light candles nightly to create atmosphere and ambience. I fill them with intentions and prayers, and I visualize my desires as curious little moths being pulled into my life by the glow of the flame. While I work with clients, I often light

candles to inspire calm and healing and to attract benevolent spirits who wish to work with us. The natural energy emitted from a candle flame attracts spiritual energy.

You hold in your hand a vehicle of change to help you call upon your own inner magic and elicit your desired transformation. Candles can be dressed, blessed, and empowered with the herbs, oils, and other curios that hold significant vibrations. The candle is just an energetic tool to help you align with your desire. The more intentional you are with this desire, the more potent the magic.

When working with intention candles, consider what you are working for. Your intention or desire is the heart of the magic. If you are drawing something to you, imagine the candle as a light luring your desire into your life. If you are clearing something away, imagine as the candle melts and begins to disappear so too does the block or place of resistance.

You can create so much change in your life by simply lighting a candle with intention. If you are in need of something, take a fresh candle, say a prayer/affirmation of your request, and then light the candle. Tuck your request underneath its base, written out on a piece of paper. Pour your gratitude, your desire, and your intention into the flame, feeding and fueling it. Do this nightly until your desire has come to fruition.

Those who are in spirit can see the glow of a natural light. If someone is missing from your life, whether through distance or passing, carve their name into the soft wax of a fresh candle's side. Light the candle in a private place. As the candle burns, begin speaking your feelings into the flame. Know that you will be heard in the head and heart of the person you miss.

Remember, the candle works with your actions and intentions.

Action + Intention = Results.

You must take the proper steps toward getting your desire in order for this work to be successful.

## Magic in Every Moment

Shaheen has also experienced the power of candles to connect with magic wherever he is:

> "When I travel, I love lighting candles at the local churches. There is a special energy that lives in the walls of each place, a kind of spirit that hears and helps

along your request. I have lit candles in London, Mexico, New York—in churches all over the world—each candle a special prayer gently sent into the flow of the Universe.

A sweet-scented candle burned in the evening will shift your state of mind into relaxation. Doing this nightly will be a mental cue for your mind and spirit to be at ease, soothing and calming your emotions. You will then be able to tap into the wellspring of your inner wisdom.

Write the things you wish to release from your life down on a fresh piece of paper. Light a new black candle in a private space. Begin to pour these painful feelings into this fire of transformation. As the candle burns, the stuck energy in your life is released back into the Universe to be recycled into something better.

As you begin lighting candles with intention, study how the flame dances and the wax melts. Does the flame stand tall and straight? Does it poke around, bobbing back and forth? Does it wave, sputter, or struggle to burn? These are all symbolic of the strength and clarity of your spell's intention!

## Preparing Your Candle

There are many types of candles you can work with—from pillar candles and jar candles to small tapers and tea lights. What works for you will depend on time, intention, and environment. Jar candles are especially good because they are an easy container in which to house the spirit of your desire.

Regardless of the type of candle you choose, imagine the candle as yourself, either pulling in your desire as it burns or transforming it into something new to release an old version of yourself.

You can make candle magic as simple or as complex as you'd like. If you're working with a jar candle, you can add herbs and oils to the top of the candle before lighting it. If you're using a freestanding or taper candle, you can inscribe words into the wax and then rub oils and herbs over it to imbue it with even more magical energy.

When working with a jar candle or a candleholder, you can write out your desire as a petition that is folded and tucked under the candle's base. If you'd like to inscribe your candle, simply write your name along one side and a word or phrase that conveys your desire along the other.

Botanicals hold specific vibrations or energetic frequencies that can add to your intention. You might choose to use essential oils or oil blends like those found in conjure or occult shops. You can add powdered herbs around the base of your candle or roll the oiled candle in a mixture of herbs to cover all sides.

To anoint a candle with oil, dab your fingers with the specific oil you're using, then rub from the base of the candle up to the wick on all sides, thinking of your desire and imagining it coming to you. If you were banishing or releasing something from your life, you would do the same, but rub oil from the wick down to the base.

Now you can sprinkle or roll herbs on the candle or around the base of where you are lighting it. All the while think of your desire.

**HERBS, OILS, AND STONE FOR COMMON DESIRES**

*Love: Roses, jasmine, and lavender. Rose quartz.*

*Money: Cinnamon, basil, allspice, and mint. Pyrite.*

*Healing: Thyme, rue, marjoram, and life everlasting. Citrine.*

*Protection: Anise seed, eucalyptus, hyssop, and lemongrass. Black tourmaline.*

*All-purpose: Patchouli, basil, and rose. Quartz.*

## Colors and Candle Magic

Manifesting with candles can be as simple as lighting a fresh white candle and saying a prayer, but you can enhance the power by combining other elements. You can add herbs, oils, crystals, and other talismans. A simple way to enhance the power of a candle working is to draw on the psychology and vibration of colors. Each color is a like a vibratory key. Simply learning what certain colors mean will get you started.

*White: All-purpose, purity, divinity, light, peace, healing, spirit guides, and the seventh (crown) chakra.*

*Black: Mystery, the universe, protection, wisdom, the feminine aspects of the divine, change, winter, and spirit communication.*

*Red: Passion, romance, sexuality, power, summer, anger, lust, creativity, and the first (root) chakra.*

*Blue: Communication, blessings, healing, animals, clarity, the angels, harmony/serenity, and the fifth (throat) chakra.*

*Green: Nature, spring, prosperity, fairies, healing, Mother Earth/goddess, and the fourth (heart) chakra.*

*Yellow: Confusion, empathy and telepathy, earth spirits/energy, the sun, awakening, renewal, success, power, and the third (solar plexus) chakra.*

*Purple: Psychic abilities, awareness, magic, higher power, the celestial bodies, sensitivity, understanding, higher education, crowning success, and the sixth (third eye) chakra.*

*Orange: Work, career, health, nutrition, abundance, road opening, and the second (sacral) chakra.*

*Pink: Love, friendship, healing, understanding, forgiveness, matters of the heart, and the fourth (heart) chakra.*

*Brown: Stability, hearth and home, finances, work problems, grounding, justice, karma, and letting go.*

*Gray: Protection, invisibility, fear, compromise, and neutralizing.*

## Candle Magic Tips

Before you work any candle spell, know your desire. Gather your supplies. Find a place you'd like to work your spell. Cleanse and clear your space, and get into a meditative state. Fashion your candle in whatever way you desire with herbs, oils, and other adornments. When your candle is ready, breathe into it three times with your desire and intention, adding a bit of your own essence to give it life.

## Simple Steps for Lighting Your Candle

1. Take a fresh sheet of paper and write out your desire three times, followed by your name or the names of those involved with your desire. You might create an affirmative statement to crystallize your intention.

2. Now fold the sheet of paper as small as you can. Fold toward you to draw something in or away from you to send something away.
3. Place the paper petition beneath the candle you are burning for your desire.
4. Hold your candle in both hands or gaze at it softly while concentrating on your petition, the things you wish to draw in or release. Do this for a few minutes until you feel complete.
5. Place your candle on a safe surface (a plate with tinfoil covering it works great). Light the candle, still keeping your intention in mind. Repeat aloud your intention a few times as the candle burns.
6. Allow the candle to burn down completely or for a few minutes each night until complete.
7. Should you extinguish and relight the candle, make sure to use a snuffer and to repeat your intention each time you relight it.
8. Always practice caution with fire and remember the magic is *in you*! The candle is just a tool to help you create this change.

## *Explore Magical Rituals*

### Protect Your Neck

Daily protection is a necessity. There is a lot of spiritual pollution out there. Even when the world seems to be operating perfectly fine, humans are still capable of emitting a tremendous amount of negative energy.

You'll want to keep your own energetic field clean and protected at all times. Fortunately, that's easy to do. Creating a circle of golden light around you every morning will give you "spiritual armor." Here's how to do it:

Sit quietly and close your eyes. Follow your breath in and out until you begin to feel centered. Visualize a bubble of golden light in the shape of an egg surrounding your body. As you breathe in, imagine that you are breathing in this radiant light. As you exhale, the light expands around you. Feel your energetic boundaries becoming stronger and brighter. Imagine that you are completely enveloped in this light.

If you'd like, you could state a simple intention such as "I am completely protected by golden light. Only positive energy can penetrate this golden light."

That's it—easy, quick, and effective.

## When You're Feeling Ungrounded

This simple ritual is great to do when you've been blindsided by a person or situation and feel ungrounded, stressed, and energetically depleted.

Sit with your feet firmly planted on the floor.

Close your eyes and breathe deeply down into your abdomen. Exhale completely.

Visualize a grounding cord wrapped around your waist. Imagine the cord reaching down into the earth and wrapping around its hot, molten core.

Breathe deeply and feel the security of the earth underneath your feet. With each breath, bring the energy of the earth into your body.

Know that you are grounded, centered, and supported.

## When Encountering Negative People

This color visualization breath work is perfect to do when you come across negative, difficult people throughout your day. It's a discreet and positive way to ward off bad vibes other people may be sending you consciously or unconsciously (not everyone knows they are emitting bad vibes).

Here's what you do:

As you breathe in, visualize that you're breathing in golden light.

As you breathe out, visualize that you're breathing out a cobalt blue color.

Imagine the blue enveloping the other person, calming them, supporting them, and healing them. This breath work will change even the ickiest encounter into an opportunity for healing work.

## New Moon and Full Moon Rituals

The mysterious moon has enchanted and fascinated humans since the beginning of time. After all, it controls the tides, as well as mirroring women's monthly cycles. The moon also has the ability to affect emotions. If you've ever felt "off" during the full moon, you know exactly what that means.

When you're in tune with the energy of the moon, you can connect deeply with your intuition, spirituality, and the rhythms of the world. The cycles of the moon can also be used for growth and transformation.

Lunar rituals are a potent way to create change in your life or in the world around you. By working with the moon's cycles, you can tune in, clear energy, and plant seeds for the things you want.

## THE FULL MOON

The Full Moon symbolizes ripeness—wishes and intentions set in the New Moon are now able to come to fruition. Manifestation is at hand, and the stage is set to release in order to prepare for the new cycle that begins on the next New Moon.

Rituals around the Full Moon should be centered on letting go and forgiveness. This is the time to release anything that's not working, as well as those things that no longer serve your higher purpose. This could be self-limiting beliefs, toxic habits and patterns, negative people, or projects and situations that bog you down.

When you surrender and let go, you create space for healing and new things to arrive. In order to live an abundant, healthy life, you must be able to let go of things that do not serve you.

For this ritual, all you need are paper, a pen, a candle, and a fireproof vessel.

On the Full Moon, set aside some time for reflection. Light the candle and put it in the fireproof vessel. Ask yourself: what or whom am I ready and willing to let go of? Where do I need to practice forgiveness?

Write a list of anything or anyone that you need to release and forgive. You can write as many things on your list as you'd like. Take your time with this, and be gentle with yourself. If you are having trouble forgiving a particular person, do not beat yourself up. Forgiveness takes time, and it must be authentic. You can add the person to your list, but know that if you find negative feelings arising weeks after the ceremony, it doesn't mean you failed in this. It just means you're human and still have work to do around this situation.

Once your list is complete, take a few minutes to sit with it. Breathe deeply, and envision yourself cutting the cord, letting go of the situation, forgiving that person (or yourself), and feeling at peace. Take a moment to say: thank you, thank you, thank you.

Then, turn the paper clockwise ninety degrees. Write the following over your list:

*I let go with love, light, and peace. May I be purified and cleansed, and may all persons in this situation be purified and cleansed as well. So mote it be.*

Next, fold the paper away from you two times, and then, using the flame of the candle, light the paper, put it in the fireproof vessel, and let it burn. (Be *very* careful with this. Do not do this in an area or near things that might be a fire hazard.) Once the flames die out, take a minute to send out gratitude to the Universe for the lessons learned.

Blow out the candle. Take the ashes from the paper and find a crossroads. Toss the ashes over your shoulder as you walk through the crossroads. Don't look back. It's done. You're free.

Lastly, you may want to consider smudging your space with the window open to let go of any leftover vibes that may be lingering.

## THE NEW MOON

The New Moon signifies fresh starts and pure potential. This is the time to set your intentions and plant seeds for the future. Think of it as the day when you can begin anew—and make magic happen.

The energy here is open, ready for you to fill it with your wishes and goals. It's law of attraction time, baby!

For this ritual, all you need are a sage wand, a pen, and a journal that is solely used for New Moon intention setting. Theresa has filled many of these journals over the year: When one is full, she starts a new one.

Begin by lighting the sage wand. Allow the smoke to waft around your space. Direct it to all four corners of the room, and let it drift around your body too.

Sit quietly for a few minutes, reflecting on your blessings. Take a moment to thank the Universe for all that you have, all the people in your life, and all that you are. Say thank you, thank you, thank you.

Next, begin writing your wishes in your journal. We recommend doing no more than ten at a time. Too many short-circuits the practice. What's important is that you are setting intentions that are aligned with what you want—and that feel good. Your wishes should be as specific as possible because the Universe likes that. You may also want to add "easily" to your intentions so that you are setting the stage for effortlessness.

For example, a wish about healing a relationship with a loved one might read like this: *I would like to easily mend my relationship with my sister.*

An intention for abundance might be: *I easily attract abundance into every area of my life.*

Write this in a way that feels real; you want to be able to imagine that you already have this in your life. Above all, be realistic. Setting an intention to marry a celebrity might be a waste of energy unless you're actually dating that celebrity!

Once you've written your list, sit with it for a few minutes. Visualize what your life might look like with this wish fulfilled. How might you feel? How would you act? What difference would it make? Then, say this statement: *"I trust that the Universe is working in divine timing, in the best way possible, for my highest good, to manifest my wishes."*

Let go and trust that the ball has been set in motion.

Theresa has seen the impact this practice has over time:

> **//** One of the things I like to do is look back to my old journals. I'm amazed every time at how many of my intentions have come to pass. This is a powerful practice, and once you get into a regular habit, you will invite magic into every part of your life.

## Dark Moon Ritual*

The Dark Moon is the period when the moon does not reflect sunlight toward the earth. This occurs a day or two before the New Moon arrives. The Dark Moon is not visible in the sky; when the small sliver crescent begins to come into view, that's when we know the New Moon is here.

The Dark Moon is a time for rest, reflection, meditation, and soul-searching. It's good for turning inward and asking yourself: what do I want? Use the information you gather to set your intentions for the New Moon. This day (or days) is also ideal for banishing work. What do you want to cast away: that stagnant relationship? those self-limiting beliefs? that awful argument you just had with a loved one? Expel it from your life so you can welcome the things you really want.

---

*reprinted with permission from The Tarot Lady blog

Good questions for reflecting on are:

*What am I ready and willing to get rid of?*

*What is no longer working in my life?*

*In what ways am I holding myself back from having the life I want?*

*What shadow beliefs do I need to confront?*

*What goals could I set right now?*

*What new habits and thoughts might move me toward my goals?*

*What do I want to receive?*

*What am I ready and willing to welcome into my life?*

Sit with these questions for a spell, and then journal your answers. Take a few slow, deep breaths. As you exhale, envision yourself disengaging from the things you no longer want in your life. As you inhale, see yourself receiving the things you want. Continue this breath work and visualization for a few minutes until you feel calm, clear, and ready.

This is powerful healing work—and a good way to begin generating energy for the life you want.

## *Jar Spells*

### Sweet Life Jar Spell

When things turn a bit sour, you can make them sweet again. Drawing on the power of honey or some other sweetener, you can make yourself delectable to a person or situation of your desire. Creating a sweet or honey jar comes from a long line of folk magic, where simple things are turned into effective magic. Working a sweet jar is like adding a bit of honey to a bitter cup of tea. A bit of liquid, gooey gold turns everything into a delicious treat.

A sweet jar can be created with any form of sweetener. Whether honey, syrup, sugar, jam, or molasses—whatever you have will work, and the sweeter, the better! Honey is the most common ingredient, but you can combine sweeteners if you would like! This tends to be a slower and more deliberate spell worked over time, so keep in mind different sweeteners will yield faster or slower results.

Sweet jars are worked for a number of reasons, such as love, harmony, and prosperity or to sweeten anyone or anything you'd like. Think of the jar as you or the situation you are working on. What you add to the jar is woven into the energetic story. Traditionally, this is called sympathetic magic.

Begin with a fresh jar of honey that has a metal lid. The jar will house the magic you create, becoming a container and a magnet to draw and increase your desire. Within the jar, you will add different ingredients to help add to your wish. The metal lid will allow you to burn candles on top of the jar to keep the magic going.

## ESSENTIAL INGREDIENTS

*A jar of honey with a metal lid*

*Parchment paper*

*A saucer*

*A pen*

*Magnets/lodestones*

*A candle of appropriate color*

*Oil of the appropriate type for dressing the candle*

*Incense*

*A knife or needle to carve the candle with*

*A taglock representing the person or situation being worked on (e.g., an item of clothing worn by the person)*

## A FEW TIPS

Lavender honey is optimal for same-sex partners. Clover honey brings fast action. Local honey, or honey from the area of the person whom you are working on/for, is best. Real honey is better than artificial.

### CEREMONY

Gather your ingredients on a tray. Take a ritual bath with vinegar and sea salt, lemon juice, or Florida Water prior to the ceremony. Also wash the jar, candle, and other tools. Prepare the space by cleansing it with sage, salt water, and light. Cast a circle if you feel it is appropriate, and be sure to work in private.

Now draw a circle on the parchment paper. Carefully tear it out (do not cut it). Write the person's full name an odd number of times in a column within the circle. Now turn the circle ninety degrees, and write your name an odd number of times in a column over the name of the other person.

Think of a simple phrase for what you wish to happen (how you want to sweeten the person up). Write the phrase around the edge of the circle in an unbroken ring. Do not pick up the pen. The phrase should all flow together.

Light the incense. Begin passing each item through the incense—one at a time. Pray as you are building the energy of your intention. Imagine how it feels to achieve what you want.

Open the jar, and eat a bit of honey. Say:

*This honey is sweet. (Phrase for what you are working on) will be sweeter.*

Now place the open jar on the saucer.

Begin folding the paper, folding the names in toward you. This brings the energy closer to you. As you fold the paper, you can also fold in personal items that you might like to add. Fold the paper three times.

Push the paper into the jar of honey. Begin adding other items, such as a photo, stones, oils, herbs, etc.

Place the lid tightly on the jar.

Take your candle of the appropriate color, and inscribe it with the name of the person or situation and your intention for the working. You can also inscribe symbols, dates, astrological signs, and any other relevant information. Keep it simple.

Now dress the candle with the appropriate oil. Rub oil from the base of the candle to the center and from the wick of the candle to the center. This draws energy inward to your intention.

Secure the candle to the top of the jar. Speak your intention aloud three times, and blow into the candle, setting the energy of the spell. Now you can light it. Spend time filling the flames with your attention and focus.

Let the candle burn down.

Repeat the process of inscribing, anointing, and lighting the candle every Monday, Wednesday, and Friday for as long as you need to complete the working.

If the situation is temporary, when it is over dismantle the jar and bury the contents with black salt. If you are working on someone that you need to keep sweet indefinitely, keep the jar going and continue sweetening the pot.

## Salt Protection Jar Spell

Protection and cleansing are essential practices in this fast-paced world we live in. Safeguarding your energy and keeping your vibration clear of outside influences fortify you against unnecessary blocks, hurdles, and painful situations. As with any magical practice, you must agree on every level to the intention you are working on. Magic as a Band-Aid never works out in the end. To quote Aunt Jet from *Practical Magic*, "You can't practice witchcraft while you look down your nose at it."

Salt is one of the oldest ingredients used for magical protection and cleansing. What we love about salt magic is the double duty it serves—to clear and protect! Practicing with it takes wide and varied forms, from adding salt to your bathwater to creating a protective boundary from salt; it has been used across traditions to eliminate negative energy and keep it at bay. By adding a handful of sea salt to your bathwater, you can clear your aura of unnecessary energetic debris and revitalize yourself completely. Think about how restorative a swim in salty ocean water can be.

Shaheen can affirm the power of salt:

**//** Growing up in a magical household taught me many things, but one of the simple magical acts that has been impressed upon me by my mother is drawing a line across the front threshold with a bit of sea salt and asking for protection against any kind of misfortune. Simply hold a handful of sea salt and fill it with your prayer to be safeguarded against negative intrusion. Then draw a line across the threshold of your front and back doors with it. Leave the salt there until you feel the need to redraw the line.

My whole life, I have had strange and interesting experiences with the spirit world, especially in old homes and places of historical significance. As a teenager, I was taught to fill small glass vials with sea salt, pray over them for protection against unwelcome, invisible visitors, and then place them in the windowsills of each room. Folklore says that ghosts have to count each grain of salt before entering. Regardless of how you view this practice, the idea of salt as a protective talisman is old and powerful magic!

As you move deeper into your practice and begin to distinguish between your own unique voice and vibration and the influence of outside energies, you will want to protect yourself, your home, and those within it. A wonderful practice to keep yourself safe from these psychic influences is creating a protection jar.

Jar magic for protection can be done in many ways. A very common and well-known method is called a witch's bottle. Witch's bottles were created to keep "evil" from entering your home and affecting you. To produce a witch's bottle, you would add shards of broken glass, pins, a bit of your own hair, and salt to a bottle. The premise is that evil will be caught and held tight on the jagged edges of pins and glass, while simultaneously marking your territory.

For this protection jar you will need:

*Sea salt or kosher salt*

*Dried basil, rosemary, and sage*

*A piece of fresh paper*

*Something belonging to those being protected, like a piece of hair, a photograph, or a scrap of clothing*

*A symbol for money, love, health, and spirituality (milagros or charms work well for this.)*

*A glass bottle or jar (Ginger jars or apothecary jars work well.)*

Begin by cleaning your tools with holy water, Florida Water, or simply using fresh spring water. Then write out your intention on a piece of paper. You could write something like this:

*"This home is protected and cleared of all negativity and harm, seen and unseen. Blessings upon our health, wealth, love, and spirit remain. So shall it be."*

With everything gathered together, hold your hands over the objects, close your eyes, and begin praying. You can imagine white light surrounding and imbuing each object while repeating your intention.

Now fill the jar halfway with sea salt. Then tuck your intention, your personal item, the herbs, and your representation of wealth, health, love, and spirituality into the top layer of the salt, again, repeating your intention.

With your desire clearly in mind, breathe into the jar three times to fill it with your essence and ignite the magic within. Breathing into any spellwork is a common practice. It essentially brings to life the magic you are creating by giving something of yourself to the work.

Now fill the jar up completely with the remaining salt. Repeat your intention one last time and close the lid. Place your protection jar near your front door or in a main living area. The jar acts in two ways: it draws in and filters any negative energies that come through your home, and it works sympathetically to keep you cocooned in a protective layer of energy.

If you'd like to create a protective threshold or perform a cleansing bath, you can use the salt from the jar. When you've used the top layer of salt just add more salt, always focusing on your intention.

These simple rituals will help you to cope with life's ups and downs. Pick and choose the ones you need. Use a few or try them all. Bring that magic into your life!

A bit of common sense:

Keep in mind that, although magic, Tarot, and other healing modalities can help, you still need to do the work. A proactive approach to problems is required if you want to see real-life results. That could mean taking steps to actively create change or, in some situations, asking for help.

There are also situations that cannot be easily fixed through spiritual tools. For example, a person who is living in poverty may lack access to things that could help them move out of their situation. While rituals may help create positive energy, other resources such as financial aid, job training, or assistance from relatives will do far more to alter their circumstances.

We can probably agree that most people want a home, money, food, love, health, education, and opportunity, but life doesn't always dole things out fairly. Circumstances such as oppression, illness, poverty, and lack of education or opportunity can hinder some people's ability to manifest the life they want. In those situations, all the wishing and magic in the world won't make a difference unless you get help along the way.

If you find that you are facing limitations due to financial, mental, physical, age-related, or other such things that make it hard for you to change your situation, please seek the proper help in addition to doing the spiritual work. There is no shame in asking for assistance because often it's the one thing that can really make a difference in your life.

One last thing:

You may hear people talk about the law of attraction—the belief that your mind-set creates your reality. While there is some truth to that, do know that it isn't quite that simple. There are many situations that have nothing to do with mind-set, but everything to do with things that are outside your control.

For example, stating that someone got cancer because they "brought it on" through negative thinking is not only wrong, it's also blaming the victim. This only serves to make people feel bad, which is a form of spiritual shaming and counterproductive.

Please keep a bit of common sense and compassion in your minds and hearts for others who may not be as fortunate as you.

PART THREE

# THE WORLD

## *A Focus on the Collective*

*Dear seeker and kind soul. You've done the inner work, and now it's time to focus on the world at large. The knowledge contained here will help you see what shadows are operating in the world so that you may begin to contemplate how you might bring in the light.*

*Whether you take a spiritual route or a direct one, know that your participation in the world, no matter how small or large, will make a difference.*

# 8

# What's Going On?

Okay, you've got your archetype and are ready to roll with that. Now what? The next step is to find out the current character of the energy running through the Universe. This never remains the same. Instead, at the beginning of the year, there is a changing of the guard, so to speak.

## *Calculate Year Card and Associations*

Each year is guided by the influence of a particular Major Arcana card. Calculating this card clues us in on major themes and energies at work for the year and how we can navigate the terrain and support positive efforts.

Calculate the Year Card by adding each number of the year and distilling it to a sum that is between 1 and 22.

> **Example:** 2019 would be 2 + 0 + 1 + 9 = 12, making the Year Card the Hanged Man.
>
> The Hanged Man in the positive sense would indicate a year of sacrifice, new perspectives, and faith during tough times. In its shadow aspect, it could suggest treason, giving up, unfair sacrifices. The year ahead may require each of us to make some sacrifices for the good of all. If we can find a way to do that, we may just lift everyone up. Of course, if the negative side of this card becomes dominant, we may find ourselves dealing with a shaky economy and

austerity policies that harm those who need the most help. Some people may feel as if they are being "hung out to dry" if we cut aid further.

These are merely suggestions of how the energy is flowing. It is not meant to be predictive or official. As the year unfolds, you'll get a better idea of which side of the card is operating.

For each card, you'll find both the positive and shadow side of the year, along with a suggested affirmation. Because there is no way that the year can ever be zero, the Fool will be number 22.

# 1 MAGICIAN

**Affirmation:** "We create a new vision."

**Positive:** a year for talent/innovation, use of power to transform the world for the better

**Shadow:** trickery, abuse of power

# 2 HIGH PRIESTESS

**Affirmation:** "We honor feminine wisdom."

**Positive:** feminine wisdom, interest in metaphysical world

**Shadow:** oppression of women, things being done in secret

# 3 EMPRESS

**Affirmation:** "We care for and grow our community."

**Positive:** caring for the earth and those less fortunate, mothers and children

**Shadow:** oppression and abuse of women, children, coldness, lacking care, "me first"

# 4 EMPEROR

**Affirmation:** "We take responsibility for the protection and preservation of our community."

**Positive:** authority, taking care of those less fortunate, paternal energy

**Shadow:** oppression, domination, controlling others, destroying the environment, using up all the resources, war

# 5 HIEROPHANT

**Affirmation:** "We hold space for each other."

**Positive:** emphasis on spiritual and educational, charity

**Shadow:** intolerance, dogma, religious rule, oppression through religion

# 6 LOVERS

**Affirmation:** "We are in this together."

**Positive:** focus on communication, love, brotherhood, equality

**Shadow:** sexual issues, inability to communicate or see eye to eye, selfishness

# 7 CHARIOT

**Affirmation:** "We are making progress."

**Positive:** progress, moving ahead

**Shadow:** oppression, control issues, war

# 8 STRENGTH

**Affirmation:** "We overcome hardship by hearing the other side."

**Positive:** handling conflicts, peace treaties

**Shadow:** taking over, stepping in where we don't belong, might makes right

# 9 HERMIT

**Affirmation:** "We support our community by taking care of our own well-being."

**Positive:** wisdom, introspection, focus on education and spiritual growth, peace

**Shadow:** repeating history's mistakes, not learning the first time

# 10 WHEEL OF FORTUNE

**Affirmation:** "We are in process."

**Positive:** pivotal year and many changes, both good and not so good

**Shadow:** fated events or things outside of our control (e.g., natural disasters), political change and unrest, going backward

# 11 JUSTICE

**Affirmation:** "We are doing the right thing."

**Positive:** fairness and justice for all, social justice, caring for society, laws that make change for the better

**Shadow:** unfairness, injustice, unfair laws, oppression, dictator, intolerance

# 12 HANGED MAN

**Affirmation:** "We honor and learn from the uncertainty."

**Positive:** sacrifice, new perspectives, faith during tough times

**Shadow:** treason, giving up, unfair sacrifices

# 13 DEATH

**Affirmation:** "We let go of the past and move into the future with wisdom."

**Positive:** major change, out with the old

**Shadow:** tumultuous change, unwelcomed change, limbo or resistance to change

# 14 TEMPERANCE

**Affirmation:** "We are one step closer to balance."

**Positive:** balance, peace, moderation

**Shadow:** imbalance, lack of peace, war, disruption

# 15 DEVIL

**Affirmation:** "We face the impending darkness."

**Positive:** facing our demons

**Shadow:** power struggles, oppression, hurting others for gain, evil

# 16 TOWER

**Affirmation:** "We are changing the system."

**Positive:** revolution, liberation, tear down to rebuild

**Shadow:** resistance, hostile takeover, war, fear

# 17 STAR

**Affirmation:** "We are healing our wounds and dreaming a new future."

**Positive:** hope returns, healing, caring for others, rebuilding

**Shadow:** unwilling to face reality, hopelessness, sickness, poisoning the environment

# 18 MOON

**Affirmation:** "We look under the surface."

**Positive:** instincts, facing the shadow, animal rights

**Shadow:** lacking clarity, fear, anxiety, illusions, things and people are not what they seem, being fooled, enemies

# 19 SUN

**Affirmation:** "We nurture the seeds of the future."

**Positive:** joy, success, children's issues

**Shadow:** immaturity, oppression of children

# 20 JUDGMENT

**Affirmation:** "We are laying the old to rest and welcoming in the new."

**Positive:** transition, major change, a chapter comes to a close

**Shadow:** judgmental, intolerance, racism

# 21 WORLD

**Affirmation:** "We are one."

**Positive:** success, completion, taking care of Mother Earth, global concerns, integration

**Shadow:** letting the world's problems get under your skin, world war, natural disasters, climate change, separateness

# 22 (0) FOOL

**Affirmation:** "We go into the unknown."

**Positive:** paradigm shift, moving into uncharted territory, new systems, being in-process

**Shadow:** neglecting the wisdom of the past, decline of power, losing sight of the intention/goal/objective

You have your personal archetype as well as the archetype for the year. Now what? What do you do with this information?

It's actually rather simple: determine how your energy best suits what's happening in the world—and then take inspired action. For example, if your card is the Emperor and the year is the Hanged Man, in what way might you play a leadership role? What sacrifices are you willing to make in order to ensure that others are safe? That might be stepping into a role as a community organizer in a poverty-stricken neighborhood. Or perhaps you may feel ready to join a group that provides mentoring to at-risk youth. If you're not ready to take an active role in the world, you could also choose to do what you can to ensure that your family is secure.

Let's use another example. If your card is Justice, and the year is Death, what might you do? The Justice archetype is concerned with equality for all, and the Death card symbolizes out with the old way and in with the new. This may be the year that you decide to get involved in civil rights. Instead of hoping for change, you may want to work for it directly by demanding justice for all. A Hermit archetype might choose instead to educate people by gathering information and showing ways that change could be enacted. The High Priestess may be more comfortable working behind the scenes in an organization that fights injustice.

The important thing is to recognize what best fits your energy and then working intentionally.

If you have a dual number, you can choose to operate with either archetype you've found—even moving between the two as you feel called to, as Theresa describes:

**//** My archetype is Justice, which is ruled by the number 11, but it can be reduced down to 2, which is the High Priestess archetype. When I was younger, I was involved with a small underground newspaper. I was the photographer. I had a decent camera and an interest in social justice, so I was good to go!

At the time, we were concerned with the gentrification in the neighborhood, especially the impact it was having on the homeless population. Many demonstrations and riots were breaking out, and my job was to get in there and get some pictures. I was small and nimble, which enabled me to get close to the action. It was exciting until I got arrested at a demonstration and found myself in a bullpen with a bunch of women who were there mostly on drug or assault-related causes. While I was still involved for a time, I discovered that my introvert nature preferred something less dangerous.

I'm no longer on the front lines or marching in demonstrations. Instead, my energy is better suited for sharing knowledge, helping people find a spiritual solution, and donating time and resources as I can. From time to time, the Justice archetype still shows up, but I'm far more comfortable being the High Priestess.

Keep in mind that you can try on other archetypes as you see fit. If you feel called to step into the role of the Hierophant even though your card is Strength, by all means, try it out and see how it goes. Do you think you are more effective in a different role than your Birth Card? How does it feel to try on different energies? What might you learn from stepping into a different position? How might you combine what you've learned from trying on this new archetype with your Birth Card archetype?

## *Working with the Yearly Prescriptive Affirmations*

The yearly affirmations create a positive focal point, a way to remain centered on the highest vibration of the card. There are a number of ways you can work with these.

- **Begin by noticing how the affirmation feels** when you consider what is currently happening in the world. For example, in a Hanged Man year, the affirmation is, "We honor and learn from the uncertainty." How does that resonate for you? Does it feel challenging or reassuring? Do you have trouble experiencing this energy when you think about what's going on in your country or the world? If so, take some time to sit with this and keep an open mind. Remember: affirmations are a way to rewire your own internal dialogue. Even though the Universe may be serving up a pile of crud, how you view it and deal with the situation will be vital. You can give in to the negative or combat that vibe with the positive. Affirmations help to shift the energy so you can write a new narrative. Also, they support inspiration, which is sometimes desperately needed. In the case of the yearly card, the affirmations may help you to remain focused on the higher good and committed to taking action.

- **Write the affirmation down** where you can see it every day. A sticky note on your computer monitor or bathroom mirror creates a touchstone where you can remain centered on the outcome you want to see. Every time you look at that affirmation, you are charging it with energy and, more importantly, reminding yourself to stay in the positive light, no matter what's happening out there.
- **Repeat the affirmation as often as you can.** In the morning, before you go to bed, during your meditation—it's all good. Say it aloud when you're feeling especially anxious about what's going on in the world. This will help you to remain hopeful and serve to combat negative energy—as well as bummer news in the news cycle.
- **Saying the affirmations out loud** with a group can be an empowering experience. Whether you're choosing to do regular group meditations or leading a peaceful protest, imagine how much good energy you can raise by putting out a positive message!
- **Above all, let these affirmations inspire you** to be a force for good work in the world. When we are all doing our part to be positive role models and commit to making change, anything and everything is possible—no matter how dark things may seem. We are all creatures of light, and together we can banish the darkness!

## *Journaling Exercises*

Look back at other times in history and calculate the year.

*What was going on?*

*How did the energy of the yearly archetype show up?*

*What did the shadow side look like?*

Write your thoughts in your journal.

# 9

# The Body Political

If the archetype work inspired you, you may find yourself wanting to do more. But how can you be a force for good? What does it mean to be an ally? Where can you make your voice heard? How might you run for office or find other ways to lead?

Do-gooders are always needed in this world, even when things seem peaceful. We must all fulfill our role to ensure that this planet continues to flourish. A spirit of kindness, inclusivity, and compassion brings healing.

Let's start by exploring what it means to be an activist. An activist is a person who works to ignite social change. These might be the people standing at the front lines of a protest or the ones who actively work on a campaign. Activism doesn't always need to be that obvious. Sometimes radical gestures of self-expression through art or music could also create impact. It can even mean simply educating people around you.

We can all be warriors in the fight against ignorance and darkness. Each one of us can play a part. How you show up is up to you. Even if you assume that your acts are minimal, know that they, like the wings of a butterfly, can create the storm that clears the air and paves the way for a new beginning. Never underestimate your power!

Good questions to ask yourself are: What can I do to bring change and justice in this world? How might I, in my best capacity, be a source for light in times of darkness and beyond?

The first step in becoming a force for good starts with one simple principle: listening.

# *Communication and Holding Space*

Communication is a major key to successful living. Not only do you need to clearly articulate your intentions, which means clarifying them first; you also need to listen. You must truly hear others to understand how best to be of service to them and how they can be of service to you and if the feeling is mutual.

## Communication Functions in Many Ways

How you express yourself sets the tone for interactions and partnership. It can make or break a relationship or situation. Communication is expressing what you want, need, or provide in any given situation.

Communication is a firm contract. Engaging with another person clarifies the depths of your relationship, the intention of your engagement, and where this will lead. You need to be clear on where you are coming from for yourself and to the receiver.

You are communicating with others, and they are communicating with you.

Being able to listen means truly hearing what someone is saying without preparing a response. That is secondary. Truly listening means giving the person a chance to get out their intention. You will discover what your purpose is in the whole thing. Sometimes that is to have a response. Sometimes that means saying nothing or remaining objective. Other times, this means ending the conversation because you cannot take part in it. Sometimes saying nothing at all is a loud and clear message!

Remember, communication is a two-way street. It is a relationship that can last a moment or a lifetime. It is a mutual agreement to express and hold space for each other. It comes down to where the communication will go and if it serves the highest good of all involved.

- Spoken words and written messages
- Articulation and annunciation
- Silence vs. response
- Body language and visual cues
- Listening/holding space

Listening to others, even though we may not agree with them, allows for compassion and understanding. From that standpoint, real change can manifest.

Next, it's time to stand up—and speak up.

## What's Holding You Back from Standing Up?

Standing up for what's right is a courageous act. It doesn't need to be radical, nor does it need to be a public declaration. Even so, the thought of getting involved or taking a stand may feel intimidating.

Thoughts such as "I don't know where to begin" or "I don't want to get in trouble with my family" might hold you back. But know this: every movement has to start somewhere. One only needs to look at brave people like Rosa Parks, whose simple act of refusing to give up her bus seat ignited the civil rights movement. While this may have seemed like a small act of defiance, the courage this took was immense—and it changed history.

We've seen this time and time again: one person says no, not fair, this isn't right—and does something about it. These acts, even the seemingly minute ones, add up.

If you have reservations, explore them. You might find that there is nothing to fear but fear itself. Here are a few of the common fears that might be holding you back:

> **If you feel that you can't find the time:** *If you're already overloaded with a busy life, you may be short on time. This is a concern for many of us. But you can seek easy, time-efficient ways to contribute. For example, you may sign an online petition or donate money to a cause. Even sharing a post on social media could draw attention to your cause. Look for fast ways to get involved—and then commit to doing them regularly.*

> **If you feel that you don't have resources:** *On a tight budget? No problem. Even small donations can make a change. Look at former President Barack Obama's campaign as an example. Many smaller donations helped to contribute to his campaign coffers. If you don't have a lot of cash, you may also consider volunteering your time. The more bodies getting involved, the better. After all, it may take one person to get things moving, but a whole village will bring the results faster.*

**If you're not sure which issue is the most important:** *Every issue is critical. Find one that resonates and start there. For example, that may be children's health care, disability rights, or climate change. Every one of these causes needs people. Let your heart decide, and then get involved! You may find that you have one pet issue or many. It's all good!*

**If you're worried that your family will be embarrassed or angry:** *You might have different beliefs from your loved ones, but don't let this hold you back. Remember: they have a right to their opinions, but so do you. Do not allow other people's opinions to silence yours. By the same token, be respectful of theirs. Set the example of graciousness. After all, ultimately, we're all in this together. We don't have to agree!*

**If you're physically unable:** *If you have physical limitations, you may assume that you can't participate. That's not true! There are many things you can do, such as call your representatives or speak up online by writing blog posts about your favorite cause. In some cases, for example, if you are interested in attending a demonstration, but are in a wheelchair, you may want to ask a friend to support you by giving you a lift and staying with you at the event. Ask for help as needed—and then do your thing!*

**If you live too far away:** *If distance is an issue, there are a few things to consider. You may want to gather a group of people interested in the same cause and carpool. This may be a bit of a trek, but if you pool the resources, it will make it easier on the budget. Plus, a group of people on a road trip? Fun! If this isn't your jam, keep in mind that the internet is your friend. Sharing information about the event is a way to be there . . . even when you can't.*

**If you think you're too young:** *Hey, you're never too young! Many movements were started by young people! Whether you're holding up a sign at a march or starting a fund-raising effort at your school, you can make a difference. Seriously.*

**If you think you're too old:** *See the above. Even if you're elderly, you have a voice—and loads of experience to contribute. Show up! We need our wise elders! (Psst . . . voting is a way to make your point.)*

**If you're afraid you'll get hurt:** *This is a valid fear because demonstrations can turn ugly. If you are too scared, then live events may not be for you. If, however, you still want to participate in a march or some other event, go with a group of friends. There is safety in numbers! If something violent does happen, get out of there as soon as possible. Seek help if you are injured or if you witness someone else being hurt.*

**If your partner objects:** *If your partner isn't allowing you to get involved in a good cause, there are issues with your relationship that need exploring. No one should have the right to prevent you from doing something you believe in. It may be time to sit down and discuss their concerns. Are they worried you'll get hurt? Are they concerned you won't have time for the family? Do they have different beliefs or want to be in control? Talk this out and if you can compromise, great. If they are being unreasonable, this may be time to reflect long and hard on your relationship.*

These are just a few examples of things that might be preventing you from standing up and getting involved. Know this: you're not alone. Most of us feel scared or nervous, or have real-life complications that make us feel that we cannot be effective. But we take a deep breath and do the work anyway.

You don't need to be on the front lines nor do you have to donate all of your spare change. Any action, even those that seem to be the tiniest, will have an impact.

Your involvement matters.

Take a deep breath and know that your contributions to the world are important.

## *Justice Exercise— Tarot Tools for Your Best Work to Change the World*

Our friend, Courtney Weber, author of *Tarot for One: The Art of Reading for Yourself*, has contributed a fabulous Tarot exercise for when you're wanting to change the world but are not sure what your first step should be.

Courtney explains that there is something that bugs all of us—call it the "pebble in your shoe"—that makes it hard to move forward until you stop to address it. For some of us, it's abused or homeless animals. For others, it's workers' rights. For others, it's environmental protection, fair wages, or something else. The list seems endless, but there's an immense amount of work we can do on something that absolutely breaks our heart . . . with only the tools we have at our fingertips.

But what tools are those?

To begin, take a piece of paper and create four quadrants. Label the first quadrant: *What I am good at and enjoy.* The second should be labeled: *What I am good at but don't enjoy.* The third: *What I am not good at, but enjoy anyway.* The fourth: *What I am not good at and don't enjoy.*

List as many things as you can. Don't be shy or afraid to boast! If you're good at something, list it! Your heart's cause is at stake here!

After you make your lists, reflect on the question, how can I best implement these things in the work that I do? Draw one Tarot card for each.

Courtney used her own results as an example:

// For the list of things I love and am good at, I received the Ace of Swords, which I interpret as a sharp tool for getting work done effectively. I interpret this to mean that these things I love are really helpful to my causes. Perhaps I can bake cookies for protestors or organize a fund-raiser.

For the things I don't love but am good at, I received the Sun. I interpret this to mean that I really shine in these areas. However, because the sun can also burn, I may want to limit how much time I spend organizing marches, as I'm more likely to burn out.

For the things I love but am not good at, I got the Seeker (another name for the Fool). There is potential for growth in these areas, according to this card. Perhaps if I spent more time practicing my guitar, I'd be able to contribute music during a sit-in!

Lastly, for the things I don't love and don't enjoy, I got the Ace of Wands. I see the Ace of Wands as a card of pure potential and untapped talent. As much as I loathe working with technology, maybe with more experience, I could become more comfortable with it and actually become proficient in working with it. It's always helpful to have someone who can fix the projector during a town hall meeting!

## *Politics around the Dinner Table*

Our worldview is shaped at home. At an early age, we hear our parents' concerns and their beliefs. Even if you come from a family that is apolitical, at some point, unless you live off the grid, there will be conversations around what's happening in the world. This is especially true when times are tense. How those discussions happen may determine how you feel . . . and act.

*Was your family engaged in politics?*

*If so, how did you feel about this?*

*How did your family talk about racism?*

*Did your family discuss sexism?*

*Were LGTBQ issues ever discussed at home?*

*Were political discussions at your home civil? If not, how did that make you feel?*

*Are your beliefs now radically different from the ones you grew up with? If so, why?*

*How do you talk about social issues at your home today?*

Theresa describes her personal situation:

" My interest in politics began early on at the family dinner table. Politics was often the topic of discussion, so I remember hearing my father talk about what was happening in the world. Even though I was too young to understand some of what he was saying, I knew that I needed to pay attention.

My father was a young man during the Great Depression, so he remembered all too well what it was like to be truly down and out. He talked fondly about Franklin Delano Roosevelt and how his policies changed the country for the better. In our household, voting was considered the most important civic duty you could engage in, and both my parents stressed how this was vital to our democracy.

As a teen, my politics matched my music. I discovered punk rock when I was twelve years old, and it completely shaped my viewpoints. Like my parents, I believed in democracy and lifting people up. But I also became concerned with issues such as feminism, classism, sexism, homophobia, and the plight of homeless people.

It was no surprise then when I began working on an anarchist newspaper as a young adult. The truth is my foray into that realm wasn't just based on my interest in politics; I also happened to have a decent camera. Suddenly, I found myself attending protests, taking pictures of demonstrations and riots, and engaging in activism for the homeless. It was exciting, and I learned so much.

Since that time, I've stepped away from the front lines and have instead been actively engaged in different ways: with charitable acts, staying abreast of the news, sharing information, and voting. Like my father, I raised my children to be interested in politics. Both of them have been politically active. From canvasing for candidates they believed in to protests, vigils, and contributing to worthy causes, I'm proud of how they have stepped up.

My father would have been proud too. But he might not be totally surprised because world events were, once again, talked about and debated around the dinner table when they were little. That includes the one and only time my father and I ever got into it.

As the children tried to tuck into their pork chops, I was busy arguing with my parents. This was during a particularly nasty election year when they voted against their own best interests because of something they had heard on the news. Things got a bit tense as I had to lay out how their vote was going to hurt the one thing they cared deeply about: social security, which was what my father felt was the turning point for so many Americans during that time so long ago when FDR created the very thing that would support the secure elderly life my parents then enjoyed.

This debate led to two things: my parents never voted against their best interests again, and my children learned that politics are something they need to pay close attention to because people can be hurt when the wrong leaders are in charge.

Perhaps you're interested in getting involved because you see what's happening out there. Maybe you're already doing your part. But even if you aren't and want to start doing something, know that small gestures can start turning the tide in the direction you want to see. You only need to show up and do something.

That something could be staying on top of current events so you remain an informed constituent, attending or organizing town halls with your local government, educating your loved ones, canvasing during election years, or running for office yourself. You are not too small to make a difference! Every one of us shares a part in this world, and if we can all do our best to create positive changes, think about how the world will look! We can truly move from troubled times into enlightened ones.

You are an important part of this world. Make an effort. Don't put your head in the sand or be too stubborn to look at other points of view. Start those conversations around the dinner table. Begin there. And then, get involved at the level that makes the most sense for you. We can do this!

Here are some ideas for sparking conversations during troubled times:

*If you were in charge of the country at this time, what is the first action you'd take?*

*In your opinion, what is the most important political issue right now?*

*What do you feel makes a good politician?*

*What do you think is the biggest political issue in the world at the moment?*

*Who do you think is the most influential politician in history and why?*

*What was your biggest political concern when you were younger?*

*When you think about the future of the country, what is your biggest concern?*

*What is the one thing that you think we could all do that might make a difference in the world?*

You can also consider a few pointers when discussing politics with the family:

Be aware of who is at the table. If there are differing views, you'll want to ask yourself why you want to open up a dialogue. Will it be productive? Is there a way to discuss things without heading into a shouting match? Sometimes countering views can be stimulating, while at other times, a screaming argument with your belligerent uncle isn't worth it.

Keep in mind that even with the most enlightened conversation, you may not change anyone's viewpoint. If you can accept this, the discussions could be more productive. Remember: everyone has a right to their opinion, and although you may not like it, you can find a way to respect this, even if you are against the views you hear.

Listen as much as you talk. Do not be so concerned with making your point that you disrespect other people's thoughts. Even if you don't agree, listening and asking for clarification will keep things respectful.

If you feel your temper or ego flaring, step back and cool down. If the other person is getting angry, agree to disagree and then end the conversation. While there is nothing wrong with a heated debate, if it crosses the line into vitriol, no one wins. Know when to walk away.

Also, if people are being rude, or using language that is abusive or that veers into territory that is racist, homophobic, sexist, ableist, or classist, call them out on it. Accepting different points of view does not mean condoning abusive, denigrating language. You can let them know that this will not be tolerated in your presence.

Follow these tips, and your dinner table could become the place where your family learns how to communicate and participate in democracy. Involvement in the greater good begins right at home.

## *How to Be an Ally*

What is an ally? This is a person with privilege who is willing to stand up and take responsibility to change oppressive societal patterns such as racism, sexism, homophobia, ableism, and classism. These are only a few examples of the various ways people are oppressed.

An ally recognizes both their privilege and own experiences of oppression, and even if they are not a member of a marginalized group, they work to understand them and support them in any way possible. They stand side by side with them, ready to carry weight and do the work necessary to understand, educate, and fight systematic oppression.

What is privilege?

Privilege is the unearned advantages or benefits that are granted to people who fit into certain social groups or identities. Those who have privilege are often not aware of their unearned benefits, while those who are marginalized are quite aware of what oppression looks and feels like.

Here are a few examples of privilege:

- White
- Male
- Access to money

- Heterosexual
- Able-bodied
- Cisgender

If you can identify with one of these examples, you have privilege. There are many other examples of privilege, but these are the most common.

Having privilege doesn't mean that your life is easy. You can still have challenges, but if you have privilege, you will have an easier time than someone who does not.

For example, if you're a woman, you may experience sexism. But if you're a black woman, you will experience sexism and racism.

If you're a black woman, you may experience sexism and racism, but a black disabled woman would experience both of those, plus ableism.

Got it?

That's privilege in a nutshell.

Privileged people are needed in the fight for equality! Your voice is important and you can be a crucial ally for oppressed people.

You might find yourself wondering what you can do as a privileged person and how you can be a good ally. Here are some good ideas:

- Do your part to educate yourself about systematic oppression. Read, attend lectures, spend time with marginalized folk. The more you know, the more effective you'll be.
- Spread the word! Take what you learn and educate other privileged people. This is a critical step in creating change.
- Join social justice groups and activist organizations. Get involved as much as you can.
- Ask questions and then *listen*. This is the most effective way to learn. (Psst . . . do say thank you when someone shares helpful information or their story.) Also: when you are entering the spaces of marginalized people, follow this rule: *listen more*.

- When you see oppression happening, don't stay silent, even if you are scared. Stand up and speak up! Confront it—even if that means rocking the boat!
- If you get called out for oppressive behavior or privilege, listen up. Don't make excuses or dismiss the concerns. Apologize. State what you're going to do to change things—and then do it.

## A Tarot Exercise for Exploring Allyship

Grab your Tarot cards and begin shuffling. Once you feel centered, put the cards face-down and cut them into three piles. Put the deck back together and fan the cards out. Choose one card for each prompt:

*What is my privilege preventing me from seeing?*

*What do I need to hear at this time?*

*What do I need to learn in this situation?*

*In what way can I be effective?*

*In what way can I empower and improve the lives of others?*

*How can I best support __?*

# *How to Be an Activist*

What is an activist? An activist works to create change for a cause that they care about. Anybody can be an activist. It begins by identifying where you'd like to see change—and then taking action.

There are as many causes as there are people in the world. You might be interested in climate change, school bullying, animal abuse, health care for all, or civil rights. Once you figure out where your passions lie, it's time to get involved!

The first step is to get informed. Learn as much as you can about your cause so that you can articulate your mission. Take classes, read books, visit websites dedicated to your cause. The more you know, the better.

You may choose to join an already established organization. Or you may want to start your own. Either way is fine. Organizations are great because there is strength in numbers.

Other ways to be an activist are donating your time, resources, and money. Remember that many organizations are grassroots. They often have shortages of both money and humans. If you can be present physically, do it. If not, make an effort to donate what you can. Your contributions, even if they seem small, could make a huge difference.

Social media can be an effective way to promote a cause. Share information where you can. Join online groups that support your cause. Donate money to websites. Start or sign online petitions. Make your voice known!

Petition your representatives. Remember the government works for you, the people. They need to hear from you. Call, email, write letters, attend town halls—do what you can to make your voice heard. This may be the most important part. If they aren't hearing from their constituents, your representatives have no reason to care . . . or act.

Educate other people. You can do this by speaking or writing about your cause. Get out there and share your message both online and off. The more voices raised about an issue, the more change can happen. A good example of this is the LGBTQ community, which worked hard to educate and push for marriage equality. Without a consistent, strong vocal effort, that may not have happened.

## A Tarot Exercise for Exploring Activism

Shuffle the cards thoroughly. When you feel ready, place the deck facedown, and cut it as you see fit. Put the sections back together, and fan the deck out in front of you. Let your intuition guide you as you pull a card for each of these prompts:

*What do I need to know about taking a stand?*

*How can I create change in myself?*

*How can I create change in my community?*

*How can I create change in the world?*

*Where can I take inspired action right now?*

## *How to Run for Office*

The day may come when you're ready to take the leap and run for office. Whoa! This is a big move and something that requires some thoughtfulness. For one thing, you must consider what this may mean for your life. A government role means long hours and, in some cases, becoming a public figure. Being in the public eye may seem glam on the outside, but keep in mind that your life will be scrutinized like never before. Suddenly, what you did in the past or what you're wearing today will be up for debate. If you have skeletons in the closet or are thin-skinned, you need to prepare yourself.

If you decide to go for it, you'll need to build a campaign. This means getting the right staff and raising capital. You need both if you want an effective campaign. Fundraising is never easy, but with the advent of the internet, it has become easier for average folks. When you start out, your staff may consist of family members, friends, interns, or people interested in your message. As you begin to gather steam and capital, you may be able to add people who can help your campaign.

Get clear on the issues. What are you fighting for? What does your district or country need from you? What concerns are people expressing? Do your research so you know exactly what people want from you. You can find this out in various ways, but the best method is to meet directly with people. Go to them and hear them out. Create town hall–style events to get to know your future constituents.

Develop a slogan that draws people's attention. It should be short and catchy. Create a snazzy logo and you're almost there!

Set up a website. You need a way for people to learn about you and a way for you to learn about your potential constituents. You'll also want a way to attract volunteers to canvas neighborhoods and spread the word, as well as a place to accept contributions.

Learn as much as you can about your opponent(s). Find out about their beliefs, where they stand on issues, and how they've voted in the past. This will help you debate confidently.

Contact the media and let them know you're throwing your hat in the ring. Meet and greet the public wherever and whenever you can. Go door-to-door. Hold lots of town halls. Be seen or heard from as much as possible. The more press you get, the better.

Above all, keep in mind your big why. That why should be connected to serving the people. If you hold that in your heart, you'll be the candidate that people love.

## A Tarot Exercise for When You're Thinking about Running for Office

Public office means becoming a public servant. It's not something to take lightly. If you're thinking about entering the political arena, you'll want to spend some time contemplating how this might look and feel for you. Tarot is the perfect tool for reflection!

Shuffle the cards and take a few deep breaths. When you feel ready, put the deck facedown in front of you. Cut the deck into three piles, and then put them back together any way that feels right to you. Fan the deck out and intuitively pull one card for each prompt:

*What do I need to know about leadership?*

*What does my country need at this time?*

*In what way can I serve?*

*How might being a public figure affect my personal life?*

*How might my personal life affect my public life?*

Whether you're taking a stand, running for office, supporting marginalized people, or discussing the state of the world at dinnertime, remember this: we're all in this big ole crazy world together. Everyone plays a role. We need to live together in harmony if we want to see the earth survive.

What role will you play today?

# 10

# Socially Conscious

Magic can also be an effective tool for creating social change. Energy is energy, and if there are a lot of troublesome things happening in the world, a bit of magic can shift the energy of even the darkest situations toward the light.

These rituals are designed to be worked solo, but can also be used for groups.

## *Creating an Altar for Balance, Social Justice, and Change*

An altar is a way to create sacred space as we've already explored, but will also be a venue for doing ongoing ritual work. As a physical representation of your purpose it can strengthen your intention and help you remain focused on the outcome you'd like to receive.

So let's look at what an altar is.

An altar is a space dedicated to spiritual work. It can be elaborate or simple. What's important is that it is treated as a living, breathing, sacred spot—which means it must be tended to regularly. The more you care for your altar, the more likely you'll receive the results you desire.

Here's how to set your altar up:

1. Pick a space. Depending on your circumstances, this could be a small corner in your bedroom, an entire room, the top of a dresser, or even a spot outside in the woods. It doesn't matter how big your altar is or where it's located. What matters is that it fits your needs and lifestyle and feels right for you.

2. Cleanse your altar. Once you've decided on your altar space, you'll want to purify it. You may want to wash the area down with a mixture of water and sea salt. Next, smudge the location with a sage wand. Light the bundle, and when the flames die down, let the smoke of the sage waft around your space. If you're in a room, smudge each corner thoroughly. If you're outdoors, smudge around your space in a clockwise circle. If your spot is a little corner or table, you can simply allow the smoke to drift around. As you allow the smoke to cleanse your space, set an intention for your altar. For example, you may want to dedicate your space for spiritual growth, healing, or social justice. Once your space is cleansed and dedicated, it's ready!

3. Decorate your altar with sacred objects that hold meaning for you. For example, you may want a statue of a deity, an incense burner, flowers, candles, and crystals. Your altar may be sparse with a few select items or lush and abundant with many objects. It's up to you. What's important is that your space inspires you and is aligned with the work you want to do.

A few suggestions on altars for social justice/change work:

1. You may want to include objects that symbolize your cause. For example, you may want an image of a beloved dog for animal rights or a picture of a hero such as Martin Luther King Jr. for civil rights.

2. For some situations, you may want to set up your altar for ongoing work with a candle that remains lit. In this case, you would light a new candle with the flame of the old one before it burns out. This is recommended only if you keep it in a fireproof vessel and are able to tend to it. A nosy cat could set your home on fire if they are not monitored. Another (safer) option would be a flameless, battery-powered candle.

3. If your work involves binding, you may also want something to represent the person or situation that you are trying to contain. This could be an image or you could write a petition on a slip of paper. That petition could read like this: "I want poverty lifted from the world. May all people be fed, clothed, sheltered, and with adequate access to fresh water."

## *Working with Your Altar*

Working with your altar could mean sitting in quiet meditation daily as you focus on your intention. Or you may decide to come to your altar for particular work and, when the work is done, leave it until you see the results you want. In some cases, you may choose to do a combination of meditation and ritual work. Some people even like to keep multiple altars for different workings. There is no right or wrong. Pick what makes the most sense for you.

### Ritual for Justice

Use this ritual when you desire justice, whether for personal reasons or to combat social inequity.

You'll need:

*A brown candle. Brown candles are always used in cases involving justice. Purple can be used in situations around financial justice.*

*Patchouli oil*

*An X-Acto knife*

*A sage wand*

*An abalone shell*

Light the sage wand and allow it to burn for a few minutes. Blow it out and then pass the smoke over your body, the environment, and the candle. Next, use the X-Acto knife to carve the name of the situation as well as the persons involved into your candle. For example, if you are experiencing a situation yourself, you may want to carve your name, the name of the other person or persons involved, and the nature of the situation. That might look something like this example: Lisa Abernathy, Jill Smith, bullying. In the case of a worldly situation it might look like this: Black Lives Matter, Racists, violence against black people. Also carve the symbols of Jupiter and Libra. Jupiter is the planet connected to matters of justice and draws benevolence and fairness, and Libra is the sign that rules justice as well as legal matters.

Rub the patchouli oil over the candle while envisioning the outcome you'd like to see. Light the candle and say a prayer for justice. Let this prayer come from your heart! Sit with the candle for as long as you'd like. If possible, let the candle burn down to the bottom. If this is not possible for safety reasons, snuff the candle out with wet fingers or gently blow the flame out and resume the working once a day until the candle is done.

## Prosperity for All

This ritual is so simple it can be done on a regular basis. The intention here is to create a vibe of abundance for all.

You'll need: *Dimes*

Take the dimes in your hands and bless them. Use this intention: "May these dimes bring good fortune and prosperity for whoever finds them." Then, randomly leave these dimes anywhere you'd like. You might want to leave one on the ground outside a library, on the shelf at the grocery store, at a crossroads near a gas station—wherever you like. This simple act spreads a vibe of abundance for you, but also for the lucky recipient who finds the coins.

## Prosperity for All Part Two

The homeless population is staggering. With rising housing costs and issues like addiction and an unstable economy, many people are finding themselves on the street or one paycheck away from it. It's not uncommon to see homeless people begging in many cities.

One of the kindest things you can do for someone who is down on their luck is to give them something. It doesn't need to be much. Even a few coins or a sandwich may be appreciated. But before you give, take a moment to bless the money or offering silently. Then, when you give your offering, be sure to smile and say, "Bless you." This sends a positive vibe to this person.

If you live in a city where there are a lot of homeless folks, take a handful of coins and bless them before heading out the door. You'll be ready to give and send positive energy to all you encounter.

## *Group Magic: How to Organize a Candlelight Vigil*

You may have seen candlelight vigils on the news or perhaps in your neighborhood. These are events where people come together around a cause, injustice, or important anniversary to show their support. This is often an effective way to spread a message and to offer encouragement and nurturing energy, especially after a tragedy.

There is also something quite magical about people coming together this way. A group standing together with candles lit not only draws attention to a cause but also raises the vibration surrounding it. Think of it as a public ritual for peace.

Here's how to organize your own:

Once you're clear on what the focus of your vigil will be, it's time to decide on a date. You may pick your date considering a favorable time of the year or, in the case of an anniversary, on a specific day.

Next, you'll need to find a public location such as a park, community center, or in front of a government building such as city hall or the local courthouse. You may also need to decide on an alternate location in the case of inclement weather. Some locations may require a permit. Be sure to check first.

Gather your supplies. You can find inexpensive candles with paper drip protectors online or at your local church supply or hobby store. Make sure you have plenty on hand in case you get a large turnout. If you're concerned about safety, you may also want to consider cheap electric tea lights. These can work just as well. If you are making banners and placards, you'll also want to visit a store that sells art supplies. For example, you may want to head down to your local art, stationery, or dollar store for poster board and markers. Get creative here and make signs and banners that will catch attention!

Decide on how your vigil will proceed. Will there be a walk through a neighborhood toward a specific destination? Will there be speakers of any sort? Will there be singing, prayer, or poetry? Or will this be a silent vigil? Be sure to organize your event so that it flows smoothly.

Get the word out by posting your event on social media or contacting your local media. You may also want to hand out flyers around town. Share the news as widely as you can so your vigil is well attended.

The day of the vigil, be sure to arrive early to set things up. You'll want to be as organized as possible so that things can run smoothly. This includes handing out signs and candles and showing people where to go. Once it's time, start out with an introduction, set an intention, and from there, light the candles. Then let the magic begin!

## *Group Moon Rituals for Social Change*

If want to get the Universe's attention, nothing is more potent than working with a group. Better yet, align your ritual work with the moon. When you combine many voices, focusing on a desired outcome with the moon as a backdrop, you're adding an extra layer of magical oomph!

### Full Moon Ritual

The Full Moon is the right time for any sort of clearing work. If you've experienced violence, trauma, oppression, or negativity in your neighborhood—or if there is an ongoing world situation such as a war—this can generate a negatively charged atmosphere. Such energy can lead people to depression, getting overwhelmed, numbing, or giving up. "What's the point?"

Gathering a group of people to banish this energy can shift things and create the space for positive change.

Here's what you need:

*An outdoor area where you can safely have a bonfire*

*Sage wand*

*Paper and pens*

One person will agree to lead the group.

Light the bonfire. Using a lighter, light the sage wand. Walk around the fire in a counterclockwise circle, allowing the sage smoke to waft where it will. Once this has been completed, put the sage wand into a fireproof container or simply throw it in the bonfire.

Sit in a circle quietly around the fire. The participants should begin writing down the things, people, and situations that they are ready to release. They can choose one word or perhaps short sentences. For example, they might write "domestic violence" or "bullying." Once everyone has written their petition, the petitions are thrown into the fire. Participants can sit quietly for as long as they'd like.

Before completing the ritual, each member should take a moment to give thanks for something. Always replace what you release with gratitude. This ends the ritual on a positive note.

Extinguish the fire safely and move on. Do not look back.

## New Moon Ritual

This is a creative and fun way to imbue positive energy and good intentions into the world.

Here's what you need:

*Markers*

*A watermelon*

Gather your people and head down to a beach under the light of the New Moon. The ocean is ruled by Yemaya, the Yoruban mother goddess, a protector of children. Watermelons are her preferred offering; they are sacred to her.

Once at the beach, begin searching for rocks. Once everyone has a rock, each member of the group can use the markers to write positive affirmations and intentions on their rock. These can be as simple as "world peace" or perhaps something more direct, such as, "I want justice for my brother, who was murdered." When everyone has adorned their rock, they should take a minute to sit quietly with their rock, visualizing what they want.

Then, take turns throwing the rocks into the water, trusting that the Universe is listening and the great mother Yemaya will hear the petitions. Finally, toss the whole watermelon into the water as an offering.

## *Using Tarot for Intention-Setting*

Tarot cards aren't just for divination. They can be used for manifestation. The pictures on the cards, when utilized in a magical or meditative way, can provide a visual aid or focal point. Like Tarot's Magician, when you put your attention toward your goal, your will can bring the results you desire.

Here's how to make magic happen with a Tarot deck:

1. You'll need to pick a card to represent your intention. That means you need to spend some time thinking about what you want first.

2. Once you're clear on your goal, thumb through your deck until you find the card that best represents your desire. Do you want to let go of the past? The Fool might be the card that resonates the best. Are you looking for financial growth? You might choose the Ten of Pentacles. Is a new job the thing you need the most? Then pick the Ace of Pentacles. The same thing applies if your ritual involves worldly concerns. For example, if you're looking for an end to war, you might choose Temperance. If your intention is healing the environment, the World or the Star could make sense. Again, look for what feels right and is centered on the outcome. You don't want to pick something that symbolizes the current situation; instead, you want to move past that to the manifestation of the new situation you are working toward. For example, if you want to put your energy to ending a war, the last thing you would pick is the Five of Swords!

3. Now it's time to create a ritual with the card. Set the card on your altar in a place where you can easily see it. You may want to light a candle or burn some incense. Or you may wish to write a petition on a piece of paper, such as: "I want world peace." Surround your card with sacred objects or keep it simple. It's up to you. The main thing you want is to be able to stay focused on your outcome.

4. Meditate on the card. Visualize the outcome that you want. Look deep into the symbols and see yourself or others involved, acting out the energy of this card. Sit as long as you'd like. When you feel as if you have absorbed the card into your bones, say thank you three times and finish. You can choose to do this once or you

may wish to repeat the ritual at the same time for a few days in a row. Build the energy and trust that the Universe is working with you!

5. After your ritual is complete, you may want to carry the card with you or put it in a place where you will see it every day. You may also want to create a screenshot of the card and keep it as your cell phone's lock screen so that it's always with you! Remember that focus is what creates results. The more you see the image, the more likely you'll keep your intentions brewing and the magic flowing!

## *Get Your Inner (Political) House in Order*

This ritual comes from Briana Saussy, author of *Making Magic: Weaving Together the Everyday and the Extraordinary.*

As interest in magic grows stronger and more people feel called to create rituals and ceremonies that can make a difference in their lives, there has also been a renewed focus on political magic. This is not a new idea. During World War II, witches and magicians in England performed public rituals to avert German forces from occupying their lands, and a quick glance at organizations dedicated to intelligence gathering will reveal more than one magic-making mystic employed in the ranks of spies. Today many who feel called to the magical arts have strong political beliefs and quite a few are activists who take to the streets in order to make their stand and have their voices heard. So it is natural that the question of how to support ourselves magically when we engage in politics at any level comes up.

While there are many excellent rituals and ceremonies to assist us in wise and effective political engagement, one of the most essential elements is often overlooked. Martin Luther King Jr. referred to this as self-purification, and it is the third of his four steps for an effective, nonviolent campaign. I refer to it as getting your inner (political) house in order.

This is a simple ritual that relies on nothing more than your breath and about five minutes of your time. I recommend that those who are going into any kind of political action perform this rite first, but this can also be practiced on a daily basis by everyone who feels deeply affected by politics and social justice concerns.

## Ritual to Get Your House in Order

**INTENTION**

The intention of this ritual is to support each individual in seeing themselves and their motivations with clarity, discernment, and compassion.

**PROCESS**

Take in a deep breath, feeling it move from the soles of your feet to the crown of your head.

As you breathe in, allow yourself to consider what your motivations are for whatever political engagement you are about to engage in.

Feel into these motivations and take as long as you need. You might need to exhale and then inhale again several times before you have felt into all of them.

Exhale completely, accepting whatever has come up.

Now, take a moment to consider what your goals are. What are you hoping to accomplish with this political engagement?

For example, if you are about to survey the day's headlines, is the goal to walk away more informed or to have some witty or snarky remark ready to go on your social media feed?

Allow yourself to take a few moments to look at both motivations and goals and discern if there are any that need to be eliminated in order for your political engagement to be of greatest benefit and effectiveness.

Breathe in a blessing on yourself.

Exhale and as you do so release any goals and/or motivations that are not for the highest benefit and effectiveness.

Take a final moment to feel how aligned you now are in feeling, thought, and body.

It is from this place that your actions and your voice will carry their truest power.

## The Four Cs—"How to Live a Diamond Life in a Coal World"

This Tarot wisdom and ritual come from V. Readus, of Red Light Readings.

Let's face it. Shit is rough out here these days, and I do mean *rough*. With dictators on the rise to everyday people having to fight for fundamental rights and civil liberties, the world is seeing and experiencing a very dark time. While I am a lover of the dark, I do not relish the fear, anxiety, blatant racism, sexism, or hatred that is becoming a new normal in today's society as it relates to my fellow BFF Collective or me. Given my passion and purpose in this lifetime, it is my duty to care for self to make the greatest impact in continuing to help take care of others.

Being an empath, it's a given for me that the energies of others inevitably sneak up and try to seep into my conscious actions. My very presence then becomes a traveling drive-in, and my double features are the ability to project the fearful essences of others into my own path and then negatively influence anyone that may cross it. As the Tarot BFF, I have been asked how I am able to navigate the oppressive soot of this "coal" world while maintaining a presence of optimism and hope, to deliver clarity that rivals the most well-known and sought-after gemstone known to man. My answer—the Diamond Life Ritual.

Like the "Four Cs" of diamond acquisition—cut, color, clarity, and carat—the Diamond Life Ritual abides by four Cs as well—cleansing, cards, candles, and crystals. Starting with a bundle of sage or a stick of palo santo, I smudge every corner of my living quarters while chanting, "Clean and clear, no negativity here." Once I have finished inside my home, I take special attention to smudge my foyer, front door and doorframe, and the area right outside my front walkway.

When smudging these areas, I converse with the Universe/Divine, asking for protection for myself and anyone that crosses the threshold into my home. I make sure to include that if there is any negativity attached to myself or a guest, it be stopped at the walkway, dissolved into the air, and carried away. No one wants to walk into an energetic funk cloud! After smudging, it's time to dig into the cards, and I have created the Diamond Spread (on page 258) to tease out problematic energy that may have attached itself and find out how to release it.

Start by laying out the Star card. As the focus, it is the optimism and revitalization that we are hoping to embody and share. Cards 2–5 surround the Star to create a diamond.

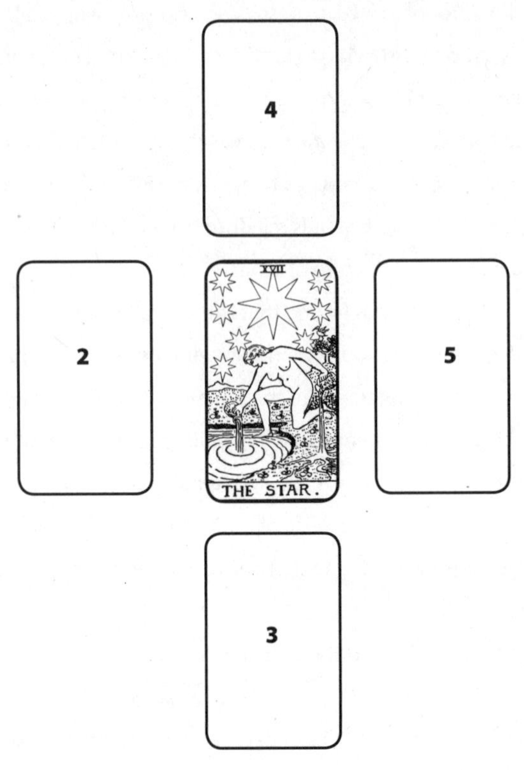


*Card 2 – Carat – The problematic energy. The heavy spiritual/emotional/mental weight that is being carried.*

*Card 3 – Cut – What is being withheld. The energy that is shaping us internally.*

*Card 4 – Color – What is being projected. The energy we are using to color our world.*

*Card 5 – Clarity – The aha moment; the brilliance. The energy we can use to shine.*

After journaling my thoughts, I take card 2, the Star, and card 5 and place them in order on my altar with a white candle for peace. Using the insight gleaned from card 5, I gather a crystal or two that coincide with the energy presented and mix in a couple more for protection, love, and balance.

I usually leave the "Prescription for Peace" on my altar until the candle burns out and then carry the stones as "medicine" to keep me well as I continue to do my part to help others strive and thrive. It is noble to want to help your fellow man and/or woman, but making sure your energy is up to snuff and able to handle the troubling times of today is your number one priority.

Diamonds are a girl's best friend, and your BFF will never steer you wrong.

## Welcoming Justice with the Tarot Knights

Lastly, this Tarot practice comes from our friend Carolyn Cushing.

Carolyn has a long history with activism and Tarot: I have been seeking justice inwardly and outwardly for at least thirty years and really, probably, most of my fifty-one years here on earth. Inwardly, I have sought self-knowledge and spiritual growth—what I call soul-tending and believe is a vital foundation for Justice—especially through the Tarot (the Justice card appeared in my first reading in 1994!), nature awareness, and taking inspiration from the world's mystical traditions. Today, I weave these strands together at Soul Path Sanctuary. This inner work has given me strength, grounding, and perspective for doing outwardly directed justice work of administrative support for peace and justice organizations; doing research and developing curriculums for bringing heart and strategy and undoing oppression work into social change; organizing gatherings and strategy sessions for communicators working for justice at grassroots and national levels; and raising lots of money for all these things along the way. Right now, I am working with neighbors in my town in a volunteer group on immigrant rights issues and transparent city government.

### JUSTICE AT THE HEART OF THE TAROT

The Major Arcana can be seen as the central suit of the Tarot surrounded by the elemental suits. In the English tradition, Justice is the eleventh card of the Major Arcana with ten cards before and ten cards afterward; it is the center and turning point of the sequence. From this perspective, we see Justice is at the heart of the Tarot, calling us to live out its wisdom in the world.

Justice is essentially *collective*. Justice is made manifest through laws, exists within groups and institutions (government, religion, and economy, for example), and is reflected in social and cultural expression.

The essential ideals of justice are *truth* and *balance*. Like all the Major Arcana archetypes, Justice and its ideals raise the elemental energies of fire (felt in the fire of the cells of each living being, reflected in a *respect* for all people, creatures, plants), water (flowing from the womb of earth's birth and our own birth, reflected in *care* for the oceans, streams, drinking water), air (giving us our breath and our words, reflected in *right speech* that serves connection rather than division), and earth (holding us all, reflected in *reverence* for the land on which we walk, that gives us our food, that nurtures our bodies).

While the work of justice can be inner-directed or outer-directed, the ultimate goal is to make the ideals of justice manifest in the world. Inner-directed justice work—such as spiritual practice, reflection time, training the mind as through meditation—serves the development of self-knowledge and resilience that are needed for effective action.

Action taking for justice happens through multiple channels.

- The **inside channel** works within institutions to uphold, advance, or repair ideals of justice. Examples could be acting as a member of a city council or school committee, becoming a civil rights attorney, working for marriage equality. (An air-inspired channel.)

- The **outside channel** watches the institutions and gives them feedback on how they are doing upholding justice and speaks loudly when justice is violated. Some examples would be the Women's March, calling legislators, supporting an immigrants' rights group, being a journalist. (A fire-inspired channel.)

- The **new channel** builds new institutions and spaces aligned with principles of justice. Founding/supporting a food co-op, starting a coven, creating alternative currencies or time banks, and restorative justice programs would be examples of this. (An earth-inspired channel.)

- The **relationship channel** reaches across the boundaries of difference to create connections that support justice. Some examples of this are Muslim-Christian-Jewish dialogue groups, truth and reconciliation commissions, listening to your uncle who has very different views from you at Thanksgiving. (A water-inspired channel.)

Most of us will find that we are more comfortable within one or two channels. Where is your comfort zone? While we don't have to work within all channels, we are still called to respect work happening in other channels. *All the channels together create a necessary balance.*

Within these channels, we all have a contribution to make for tipping the scales toward justice. The good news is that we don't have to do everything ourselves. Instead we can take on the tasks that align with our personal reality—what we are drawn to, understand, are skilled at, see as most necessary—to guide our actions. Moving from this place of strength allows us to act with balance and not burnout.

The elemental associations and images of the Tarot's Knights (sometimes known by other names such as Explorers, Knowers, or Sirens, for example) provide guidance for finding your right action to take in service to Tarot's Justice:

**Fire Knights** *(most commonly associated with the suit of Wands) inspire, by asking people to talk about and reflecting back their highest dreams and long-term visions; creating art, from poetry to picture and from song to skits; gathering people in large groups and marches to feel the power of the group and keep the heat on those in power.*

**Water Knights** *(most commonly associated with the suit of Cups) nurture and show compassion, including by ensuring good meetings and group process through facilitation; offering hospitality (food, child care, setup) for events, actions, and meetings; helping justice seekers work through feelings related to their work.*

**Air Knights** *(most commonly associated with the suit of Swords) strategize, including by laying out logical steps for achieving goals, leading planning sessions, crafting communications for clarity and to reach specific audiences.*

**Earth Knights** *(most commonly associated with the suit of Pentacles) ground* *and endure, including by raising money, persisting in calling legislators over and over again about the same issue, administrative and logistical support (getting out mailings, doing accounting, arranging for permits, setting the meeting place, maintaining the database).*

To meet your Knight guides who will inspire you to quest for Justice, here is a Tarot process to do as outlined or modify based on what your intuition guides you to do.

## SELECT YOUR DECK

If you have one Tarot deck, the choice is easy. If you have more than one deck, choose the deck that has the images of Justice and the Knights (or those cards that correspond to Knights—if you are using a Rider Waite Smith deck, yes, use the suit cards titled Knights) that inspire you the most. Even if you are at an age or time in your life when you feel more like a Queen or a Page, use the Knights for this process. They can help you find your right action, though when you do it in the world, you may still do it in a Queenly or Page-like way.

## INVOKE JUSTICE

Gazing on your Justice card you may want to say these words aloud.

*I welcome justice into the center of my heart, my mind, my spirit.*

*May the fire of your being inspire me to believe your beauty can shine forth in our world.*

*May the flow of your being purify and release me from wounds that come from the places where you are violated.*

*May the breath of your being pass through me and form on my lips words of wisdom.*

*May the endurance of your being aid me to persist in serving you.*

*May I hear your truth. May I know your balance. May I gather your wisdom.*

*Welcome, Justice.*

### ARRANGE YOUR KNIGHTS CARDS

By chance or choice, arrange your cards in a line with the first card being your lead Knight.

If you are working by chance, simply shuffle the four cards facedown until it feels right to stop and line them up. If you are working by choice, allow the images to guide your placement. Let the first card down be the Knight that most captivates your attention, that calls out to you in a positive way. The second card is also very appealing. The third card may or may not speak to you that much. The final card is your least favorite.

The first Knight—your lead Knight—is your guide to outer action. Check the descriptions of Knights we've already shared and see what kinds of actions are suggested. What passions and skills do you have in this area? What actions do you already take? What actions are a stretch but things that would help you grow? What channel (inside, outside, earth, or relationship) would you like to do this work in? Write down one to five actions you would like to take within a set amount of time (a week, a month, or a year) inspired by this card to serve justice.

The second Knight is the partner to the first card, supporting the action-taking you just identified. This card may show the inner work—such as a spiritual, creative, or self-care practice—that you do to keep in balance so you can do the outer work. From what you know about the elemental energy of this Knight or through reading over its description, what inner work is suggested? What commitment do you want to make to this work during the time period you set for action-taking?

The third Knight can represent what you do to support others in their justice work. This isn't work you do yourself, but that is possible because of the help you lend to others. This can also be work that you do occasionally because it is needed, but you don't do it as your main responsibility. We don't often give ourselves credit for this actually being the work of justice, but as you contemplate this Knight, acknowledge what your support of others makes possible.

The fourth Knight is the work you leave to others. Remember, you don't have to do everything. This Knight shows work that you can say no to because it doesn't play to your strengths or is beyond your capacity right now. You may want to make a list of one to five actions that you will let yourself say *no* to during the set time period. While you don't do this work, you recognize that it needs to be done and are grateful that others are doing it.

Use this structure as a support for meaning-making, not a straitjacket. If odd but strongly intuitive ideas come up about taking actions for justice while you are looking at any of these cards, incorporate them into your planning.

## TAKE ACTION AND KEEP CHECKING IN WITH THE TAROT

Do your best with the actions that you have outlined. For help with assessing your progress, return to the Tarot and ask for guidance, either by pulling cards from the whole deck or reconnecting with your Justice and Knight images. Be careful when judging your own success or failure. The work of justice is constant and ripples over long periods of time in unexpected ways. A big perceived failure may lead to a change in direction that brings forth something new and more needed. A seemingly small success may have a powerful impact that you may never even see. The Knights live within the now using their elemental energy to keep them moving forward. May they keep you inspired!

***A Sources and Resources Note:*** This work is most directly inspired by the weaving together of the Tarot's elemental structure and change-making models as described in Joanna Macy's *Coming Back to Life* and Linda Stout's *Collective Visioning*. The elemental Knights work is inspired by The Tarot School's Elemental Array process.

*Let this book be the first step in your revolution and let's change the world.*

Blessings,

Shaheen and Theresa

# Resources

## *Tarot Books*

*Everyday Tarot: A Choice-Centered Book* by Gail Fairfield

*Holistic Tarot* by Benebell Wen

*Learning the Tarot: A Tarot Book for Beginners* by Joan Bunning

*Modern Tarot* by Michelle Tea

*The Secret Language of Tarot* by Wald Amberstone and Ruth Ann Amberstone

*Seventy-Eight Degrees of Wisdom* by Rachel Pollack

*The Tarot Coloring Book* by Theresa Reed

*Tarot for One: The Art of Reading Tarot for Yourself* by Courtney Weber

*The Tarot Handbook* by Angeles Arrien

*Tarot Wisdom* by Rachel Pollack

*365 Tarot Spreads* by Sasha Graham

*21 Ways to Read a Tarot Card* by Mary K. Greer

*Who Are You in the Tarot?* by Mary K. Greer. This book covers Tarot's Birth Cards in depth.

## *Tarot Decks*

The Black Power Tarot

The Crystal Unicorn Tarot by Pamela Chen

The Dreaming Way Tarot by Rome Choi and Kwon Shina

Dust II Onyx Tarot by Courtney Alexander

The Fountain Tarot

Gaian Tarot by Joanna Powell Colbert

The Lunar Nomad Oracle by Shaheen Miro

Rider Waite Smith Tarot

Robin Wood Tarot by Robin Wood

The Spolia Tarot by Jessa Crispin and Jen May

The Starchild Tarot by Danielle Noel

The Wild Unknown Tarot by Kim Krans

The Wildwood Tarot by John Matthews, Mark Ryan, and Will Worthington

## *Books on Magic and More*

*Dodging Energy Vampires: An Empath's Guide to Evading Relationships that Drain You and Restoring Your Health and Power* by Dr. Christiane Northrup

*The Enchanted Candle* by Lady Rhea

*Enchantments: A Modern Witch's Guide to Self-Possession* by Mya Spalter and Caroline Paquita

*Energy Muse* by Heather Askinosie and Timmi Jandro

*Everyday Crystal Rituals: Healing Practices for Love, Wealth, Career, and Home* by Naha Armády

*High Magick: A Guide to the Spiritual Practices that Saved My Life on Death Row* by Damien Echols

*Inner Witch* by Gabriela Herstik

*Light Magic for Dark Times: More than 100 Spells, Rituals, and Practices for Coping in a Crisis* by Lisa Marie Basile and Kristen J. Sollee

*Living in Gratitude: Mastering the Art of Giving Thanks Every Day* by Angeles Arrien and Marianne Williamson

*Making Magic: Weaving Together the Everyday and the Extraordinary* by Briana Henderson Saussy.

*Protection and Reversal Magick* by Jason Miller

*The Spirit Almanac: A Modern Guide to Ancient Self-Care* by Emma Loewe and Lindsay Kellner

## Books on Activism

*Citizen's Handbook to Influencing Elected Officials: Citizen Advocacy in State Legislatures and Congress: A Guide for Citizen Lobbyists and Grassroots* by Bradford Fitch

*Everyday Activism: A Handbook for Lesbian, Gay, and Bisexual People and Their Allies* by Michael R. Stevenson and Jeanine C. Cogan

*Grassroots: A Field Guide for Feminist Activism* by Jennifer Baumgardner, Amy Richards, and Winona LaDuke

*How I Resist: Activism and Hope for a New Generation* by Maureen Johnson

*So You Want to Talk about Race* by Ijeoma Oluo

*Stamped from the Beginning: The Definitive History of Racist Ideas in America* by Ibram X. Kendi

*Unladylike: A Field Guide to Smashing the Patriarchy and Claiming Your Space* by Cristen Conger and Caroline Ervin

*Uprooting Racism—4th edition: How White People Can Work for Racial Justice* by Paul Kivel

*When We Fight, We Win: Twenty-First Century Social Movements and the Activists that Are Transforming Our World* by Greg Jobin-Leeds and AgitArte

## *Where to Go for Help*

**Crisis Text Line**

*www.crisistextline.org* / text 741741

Send a text anytime, 24/7, and a trained counselor will listen to you and reply. It's totally free. Text and get support if you're struggling with anxiety, depression, suicidal thoughts, or any type of emotional crisis.

**Suicide Prevention Lifeline**

*https://suicidepreventionlifeline.org* / 1-800-273-8255

Call to get help anytime, 24/7, and a volunteer will listen and assist you in settling your nervous system and bringing you back to a calmer place where you can think clearly.

**TalkSpace**

*www.talkspace.com*

Get set up to text and chat with a licensed therapist. This is professional therapy that's affordable and convenient. You don't have to get dressed, drive across town, and find parking. There's a real therapist right in your phone!

**Meetup**

*www.meetup.com*

If you're feeling depressed or hopeless, please don't isolate yourself. Try to get out into the world at least once a week and connect with fellow human beings. If you feel lonely, go to Meetup and find a Tarot meetup, a book meetup, an astrology meetup, or a gathering for whatever other topic interests you.

# Acknowledgments

We both want to express our gratitude to Kathryn Sky-Peck and the good people at Weiser for helping to make this book come to life.

**Theresa would also like to thank:**

Shaheen Miro for being such a wise and trustworthy partner in this project. You are wise beyond your years.

Mary K. Greer and Rachel Pollack. You have both blazed trails in Tarot and lit the way for so many of us. My work would not be possible without your wisdom.

Megan Lang for your sharp mind, editing skills, and compassion for all living things. Your big heart is appreciated.

Big love to Alexandra Franzen for your marvelous suggestions. You are amazing.

Deep bows to Damien Echols and Lorri Davis. I've learned so much about fighting for justice from watching you both.

Gratitude to Briana Saussy, Carolyn Cushing, V. Readus, Courtney Weber, Joanna Powell Colbert, Danielle Cohen, Fabeku Fatunmise, Chris Zydel, Heatherleigh Navarre, Andrew McGregor, Georgianna Boehnke, Hilary Parry Haggerty, Ethony Dawn, Jenna Matlin, Melissa Cynova, Benebell Wen, Jessica Schumacher, Simone Salmon, Al Juarez, Connie Kick, Guy and Jackie Dayen, Suzi Dronzek, Ruth Ann and Wald Amberstone, Gabriela Herstik, Donnaleigh de la Rose, and all the other friends who've supported me through thick and thin. There are many more of you—too many to name. Know that you're in my heart, always.

Gratitude to my yoga students and Tarot clients. It's always my honor to serve you.

Thanks to my children, Megan and Nick, the two most tolerant human beings I know.

And major thanks to my husband, Terry, for believing in me and supporting me through long days of writing, edits, and lost manuscripts. You make this all possible.

**Shaheen would also like to thank:**

Theresa Reed for her love, support and wisdom. I am honored by this collaboration.

Valorie Rossi and Patricia Garry, thank you for believing in me all those years ago. Your encouragement, guidance, and support have carried me through so much.

Immense gratitude for the Tarot Luminaries who've paved the way for younger generations. It is with great respect and appreciation that I add something of my own to the collective body of wisdom you've created.

To my mother, Dorothea Miro, I thank you for everything . . . you've shown me how to shine bright in this wild, crazy world.

And a big thanks to my clients and friends. You ask the big questions that keep this whole thing going.

# About the Authors

## THERESA REED

*TheTarotLady.com*

Theresa Reed is a Tarot veteran who's been doing Tarot professionally for thirty years. She's the author of *The Tarot Coloring Book* and has been a keynote speaker at The Readers Studio—the world's largest tarot conference. She's also been featured in places like *HuffPost, Nylon*, and *Refinery29*.

When it comes to Tarot, Theresa loves to remind people that the future is flexible, it's never set in stone, and your personal choices can shape a better future for yourself—and the world. Her philosophy is *"The cards tell a story, but you write the ending."* Aside from Tarot, her passions include yoga, cats, cooking, anything related to *Games of Thrones,* and spending time with her husband and kids. She lives in Wisconsin.

## SHAHEEN MIRO

*ShaheenMiroInsights.com*

Shaheen Miro is the creator of *The Lunar Nomad Oracle Deck*. He offers intuitive readings, intention setting, and energy-clearing services to clients around the world—along with magical products like aura elixirs. He writes a blog and newsletter on healing, empowerment, and transformation, and he's a columnist for *numerologist.com*. He also posts weekly *Intuitive Forecasts* on YouTube to help people shake off negative vibes and get prepared for a beautiful week.

His mantra is *"I am open and curious about life."* He loves late-night karaoke, suede platform shoes, and watching *Practical Magic* on repeat. He's a nomad and lives all over the world.

## *To Our Readers*

Weiser Books, an imprint of Red Wheel/Weiser, publishes books across the entire spectrum of occult, esoteric, speculative, and New Age subjects. Our mission is to publish quality books that will make a difference in people's lives without advocating any one particular path or field of study. We value the integrity, originality, and depth of knowledge of our authors.

Our readers are our most important resource, and we appreciate your input, suggestions, and ideas about what you would like to see published.

Visit our website at *www.redwheelweiser.com* to learn about our upcoming books and free downloads, and be sure to go to *www.redwheelweiser.com/newsletter* to sign up for newsletters and exclusive offers.

You can also contact us at *info@rwwbooks.com* or at


Red Wheel/Weiser, LLC

65 Parker Street, Suite 7

Newburyport, MA 01950